CITYPACK GUIDE TO
Milan

How to Use This Book

KEY TO SYMBOLS

✠ Map reference to the accompanying fold-out map

✉ Address

☎ Telephone number

🕐 Opening/closing times

🍴 Restaurant or café

🚉 Nearest rail station

🚇 Nearest Metro (subway) station

🚌 Nearest bus route

⛴ Nearest riverboat or ferry stop

♿ Facilities for visitors with disabilities

❓ Other practical information

▷ Further information

ℹ Tourist information

✋ Admission charges: Expensive (over €6), Moderate (€3–€6) and Inexpensive (€3 or less)

This guide is divided into four sections
• Essential Milan: An introduction to the city and tips on making the most of your stay.
• Milan by Area: We've broken the city into five areas, and recommended the best sights, shops, entertainment venues, nightlife and restaurants in each one. Suggested walks help you to explore on foot.
• Where to Stay: The best hotels, whether you're looking for luxury, budget or something in between.
• Need to Know: The info you need to make your trip run smoothly, including getting about by public transport, weather tips, emergency phone numbers and useful websites.

Navigation In the Milan by Area chapter, we've given each area its own color, which is also used on the locator maps throughout the book and the map on the inside front cover.

Maps The fold-out map accompanying this book is a comprehensive street plan of Milan. The grid on this fold-out map is the same as the grid on the locator maps within the book. We've given grid references within the book for each sight and listing.

AST
VIALE MONTE SANTO
Via Appiani
Via A G Parini
Via Moscova
Largo G Donegani
Donegani / Moscova
S Bart
Int d Finanza
Museo del Cinema
Giardino zoologico
Giardini Pubblici
Bastioni di Porta Venezia
Lecco
Ch Russa Ortodossa
S Carlo Lazzaretto
Lazzaretto / Tunisia
BUENOS AIRES
Via G Casati
Via Lazzaretto
Via F G Reti
Via G Broggi
Omboni
Via G B MORGAGNI
Via A Cadamosto
Via B Ramazzini
Piazza S Francesca Romana
Tunisia Buenos Aires
VIALE R GIOVANNA
Porta Venezia
8 Novembre
Via P Frisi
Piazza Otto Novembre 1917
8 Novembre
Lambro
TURATI
BASTIONI DI PORTA VENEZIA
Repubblica
Viale A Manuzio
Viale A Zarotto
Lazzaretto / Tunisia
Vittorio
Veneto
Vitt Veneto / Lazzaretto
Largo P Fra Bellintani
CORSO BUENOS AIRES
Turati
Via Carlo Porta
Teatro
Archi di Porta Nuova
dell' Annunciata
Palazzo Romeo
Via S Spirito
Palazzo Dugnani
Museo del Cinema
Palazzo Centro Svizzero
Villa Belgiojoso Bonaparte
Liberty-Style Architecture
Museo di Storia Naturale
Planetario
Porta Venezia
Piazza G Oberdan
Oberdan
Via Sirtori
Bixio / Pisacane
Bixio / Piave
PORTA MONFORTE
Via Nino Bixio
Cavour
Piazza Cavour
Palazzo dell' Informazione
Teatro Manzoni
Palazzo del Senato
QUADRILATERO D'ORO
Via Palestro
Palestro
ACI
Palestro
Palazzo Rocca Saporiti
Piazza E Duse
VIA VENEZIA
Palazzo Arcivescovile
Museo Bagatti Valsecchi
Museo Poldi Pezzoli
Museo di Milano
Palazzo Belgioioso
Museo Manzoniano
San Fedele
Via S Andrea
Via della Spiga
Via Montenapoleone
Napoleone
S Babila
SENATO
CORSO
Via S Primo
Via G Serbelloni
Cappuccini
Palazzo Serbelloni
Mozart
Istituto dei Ciechi
Via Vivaio
VIA S DAMIANO
Prefettura
Corso Monforte
VIALE PIAVE
Bellotti
Piazza Fratelli Bandiera
Via G Rossini
Tricolore
Piazza del Tricolore
CORSO CONCORDIA
Tricolore
Via G Mayr
Via Macedonio Melloni
Archimede
Via Kramer
VIALE PREMUDA
Marcona
Calvi
Poerio
Sottocorno
Maestri / Sottocorno
Piazza Liberty
Teatro Nuovo
S Babila
CENTRO STORICO
Corso Matteotti
Largo A Toscanini
Via Borgogna
Santa Maria della Passione
Conservatorio di Musica Giuseppe Verdi
Via V Bellini
Via P Mascagni
Corso Vittorio Emanuele II
omo
S Vito
Corso Europa
Palazzo Durini
Palazzo Archinto
Via Passione
Via Perugia
VIA VISCONTI DI MODRONE
BIANCA
Via Donizetti
Corridoni
Archimede
Piazza Beccaria
Piazza Fontana
Palazzo del Capitano di Giustizia
Largo Augusto
Largo dei Bersaglieri
Augusto
SFORZA
Palazzo di Giustizia
S Pietro in Gessate
Piazza S P in Gessate
Via C Battisti
Savaré
Via E Chiesa
Camera del Lavoro
Porta Vittoria
22 Marzo / 5 Giornate
Piazza S Maria del Suffragio
S M Suffragio
Palazzo Arcivescovile
Larga Verziere
Piazza S Stefano
S Stefano Maggiore
Palazzo Sormani (Biblioteca)
CORSO DI PORTA VITTORIA
Piazza Cinque Giornate
CORSO XXII MARZO
22 Marzo / 5 Giornate
Morosini
Via Bezzecca
Via C Folgi
Ufficio Comunale
Università degli Studi di Milano
Via P Andreani
Via S Zaccaria
Palazzo di Giustizia
Casa del Mutilato
Via C Freguglia
Via L Manara
Podgora
Via Besana
REGINA MARGHERITA
Fontana
NERO
Augusto
Anfossi
Ca'Grand
Annunciata
San Nazario Maggiore
San Nazaro in Brolo
S Sofia
Giardino Guastalla
Osp Maggiore di Milano
(Policlinico)
S Innocenti
SS Barnaba e Paolo
Soc Umanitaria
Santa Maria della Pace
Barnaba
Rotonda della Besana
Osp Maggiore
VIA FRANCESCO
Via San
Via della Pace
Via Clusone
MONTE NERO
Bergamo / Monte Nero
Monte Nero / Bergamo
Spartaco
Morosini
Bergamo / Monte Nero
Fogazzaro
San Calimero
Crocetta
Romana
Teatro Carcano
Commenda
Alfonso
Lamarmora
Curtatone
CALDARA
VIALE LAZIO
Morosini
Bergamo
CADORE
Cadore
CORSO
PORTA
VICENTINA
S Piero dei Pellegrini
Quadronno / Cassolo
CORSO ROMANA
Teatro della Contraddizione
Via della Braida
VIALE EMILIO
Monte Nero / Pier Lombardo
Via S Lattuada
Teatro
Vasari
VIALE CIRENE
Piazzale Libia
Contardo Ferrini
Via G Sigleri
Via C Crivelli
J
Porta Romana
K
L

Contents

Introducing Milan

There's an old adage, *"Milan l'è Milan"*—Milan is just Milan. The city may seem to lack the charm of other Italian cities, but if you scratch beneath the surface you will find this is a city of contrasts and hidden depths, with its own unique personality.

Milan's reputation is one of commercialism driven by market forces, and indeed it is the powerhouse of Italy's economy. But this city is not just about commercialism. Despite the Milanese modern approach to business and their trendy get-up-and-go ways, the traditional Italian lifestyle has not been totally rejected.

Milan has some of the finest churches in Italy and numerous *palazzi*, proud reminders of the city's aristocratic past. The many well-run museums offer a glimpse into the city's artistic and historic heritage. There is fantastic shopping at every level, from chic designer stores to street markets. And the style doesn't stop with fashion; even the humblest delicatessens have a certain flair.

Just beyond the *centro storico* there are other districts with a totally different feel, like the Navigli, where renovation has rejuvenated the area. You will also discover pretty parks and hidden gardens that act as tranquil oases from the hustle and bustle.

While it does have a lot of traffic and rush hour congestion, the city is a comfortable place to live and exudes a sense of well being—and, unlike some other Italian cities, the Milanese don't make excessive use of their car horns. Public transportation is excellent: efficient, clean and reasonably priced. The Milanese are happy in their own skin, unruffled and confident—busy, yes, but they always find time to be sociable.

Milan may not have the beauty of Florence, the grandeur of Rome or the romance of Venice, but it does have something very appealing all of its own.

Facts + Figures

- Area of city: 181.7sq km (70sq miles)
- Population: 1.3 million (Greater Milan: over 4 million) in 2014
- The Duomo is the third-largest church in the world
- Trade fairs in Milan draw over 4 million visitors per year

MILAN FOR FREE

There are many free museums in Milan and churches do not charge for entry, although there may be a small fee to see a specific painting. Parco Sempione is free to wander but its various attractions may carry a fee. Exploring the canal district and the old artist quarter of Brera or window-shopping in the designer streets won't cost anything either—that's if you can resist.

MILAN'S SKYSCRAPERS

The most famous of these is the Edificio Pirelli, familiarly known as Big Pirelli, which remains one of the symbols of Milan. Designed by Gio Ponti and Pier Luigi Nervi—completed in 1960—it is the tallest at 127m (417ft). This is followed closely by the Milan skyscraper at 114m (374ft), the Galfa building at 104m (341ft) and the Velasca Tower at 99m (325ft).

FASHION SHOWS

Milan was first catapulted into the limelight as Europe's fashion capital in 1971, when Italy's largest international fashion show was moved here from Florence. Today, the *Uomo* (men's) and *Donna* (women's) collections of leading designers grace the catwalks at the Fiera Milano (www.fieramilano.it) at various events held throughout the year.

A Short Stay in Milan

DAY 1

Morning Beat the crowds and start your day around 8.30 at the **Pinacoteca di Brera** (▷ 27), which has the best art collection in the city.

Mid-morning Just a short walk south is **Teatro alla Scala** (▷ 52); take a peek inside this famous opera house as you pass by. Stroll through **Galleria Vittorio Emanuele II** (▷ 48), taking in a few shops along the way. Stop for a coffee break at **Camparino in Galleria** (▷ 59) and watch the world go by while admiring the **Duomo** (▷ 46–47) laid out before you. Visit the Duomo and, on a fine day, scale the 165 steps for an unbeatable city view.

Lunch Seek out one of the tempting eateries in or around Piazza Duomo; try **Savini** (▷ 60) in the Galleria Vittorio Emanuele II or perhaps **Charleston** (▷ 59) in Piazza del Liberty, or head up Corso Vittorio Emanuele II, where there are several more options.

Afternoon If you continue along Corso Vittorio Emanuele II to Via Montenapoleone and go north, you will find yourself in the **Quadrilatero d'Oro** (▷ 28–29). Spend the rest of the afternoon exploring this network of pretty streets known as the Golden Quad—Milan's sensational shopping area—but go easy on your credit card. In the middle of the afternoon, try to work your way toward **Cova** (▷ 39), where you can rest your weary feet while you have a coffee and mouthwatering cake.

Dinner From the top end of Montenapoleone, it's only a short walk west to the **Brera district** (▷ 74). Join in "happy hour" at one of the trendy bars and then have a unique dining experience at **L'Osteria di Brera** (▷ 78).

Evening After dinner wander around the winding medieval streets of this attractive area, soaking up the lively atmosphere.

DAY 2

Morning Reserve tickets well in advance to admire da Vinci's *Last Supper* first thing in the morning at **Santa Maria delle Grazie** (▷ 72–73). If you don't have tickets, check out the beautiful church and its cloisters instead.

Mid-morning Walk a little farther down Corso Magenta to **Biffi** (▷ 78) for a quick pit-stop before heading north to **Parco Sempione** (▷ 70). Enter the park on the west side, pass the Palazzo dell'Arte and for a great view take the elevator to the top of the Torre Branca. Spend some time rambling among the lakes, modern sculptures and monuments.

Lunch There are several cafés in the park where you can have lunch or, if the weather is fine, take a picnic lunch to eat on the grass.

Afternoon Head toward the northeast perimeter of the park and pay a visit to the **Acquario** (▷ 74). Leave this underwater world behind and follow the path round to the clocktower at the front of Castello Sforzesco.

Mid-afternoon Wander down the wide, walkable Via Dante, packed with café options for a coffee break. Retrace your steps back to **Castello Sforzesco** (▷ 66–67) and go inside the massive fortress for a look around. If you have time, visit one of the Castello's interesting museums or relax in the courtyard gardens.

Dinner Take the metro from Cadorna to Porta Genova and walk south to the **Navigli** (▷ 96). Take a stroll along the towpaths on either side of the canal before dining at **El Brellín** (▷ 106) or **Al Pont de Ferr** (▷ 105).

Evening Seek out one of the increasing number of popular nightspots concealed in the side streets of this district.

Top 25

Arco della Pace ▷ 64
Triumphal arch in memory of the European peace of 1815.

Basilica di Sant' Ambrogio ▷ 82–83 A prototype for Lombardian Romantic-style churches.

Ca' Granda ▷ 44–45
Fine tribute to 15th-century Milan, now housing State University departments.

Villa Belgiojoso Bonaparte ▷ 30–31
A wonderful neoclassical gallery surrounded with gardens.

Teatro alla Scala ▷ 52
One of the world's most famous opera houses, which remains the cultural focus for the city's well-to-do.

Santa Maria della Passione ▷ 97 Exquisite art in Milan's second-largest church after the Duomo.

Santa Maria delle Grazie ▷ 72–73 Da Vinci's *The Last Supper* is here in the refectory of this significant church.

San Maurizio ▷ 71
The church exterior does not do justice to the superb frescoes displayed inside.

San Lorenzo Maggiore ▷ 86 Early Christian basilica concealing a superb interior and wonderful frescoes.

Quadrilatero d'Oro ▷ 28–29 Enticing shop-window displays at the heart of the fashion industry.

Pinacoteca di Brera ▷ 27 One of Italy's top galleries, and the focus of most visitors to the Brera.

Pinacoteca Ambrosiana ▷ 51 The oldest art gallery in Milan, founded by Cardinal Federico Borromeo.

These pages are a quick guide to the Top 25, which are described in more detail later. Here they are listed alphabetically, and the tinted background shows which area they are in.

Castello Sforzesco
▷ 66–67 A museum complex housed in an austere and forbidding fortress.

Civico Museo Archeologico ▷ 65 The story of Roman Milan told through important finds.

Corso Magenta ▷ 68 A grand, historic street where the big draw is Leonardo da Vinci's *The Last Supper*.

Duomo ▷ 46–47
The hub of the city and the world's largest Gothic cathedral.

Galleria Vittorio Emanuele II ▷ 48 A monumental arcade known as "the living-room of Milan".

Giardini Pubblici ▷ 24
A chance to relax and escape the noise of the city.

Museo Bagatti Valsecchi
▷ 25 Works of art and furniture displayed in a Renaissance *palazzo*.

Museo Nazionale della Scienza e della Tecnologia ▷ 84–85 One of the best technical-science museums in the world.

Museo Poldi Pezzoli
▷ 26 A private art collection of great Italian works.

Navigli ▷ 96 Once a hive of commercial activity and now a gentrified area of shops, bars and trattorias.

Piazza Mercanti ▷ 50
Ancient stones of the medieval market square are witnesses to Milan's history.

Parco Sempione ▷ 70
Gracious parkland unfurls around the Castello Sforzesco.

Palazzo Reale ▷ 49 The neoclassical Royal Palace, with fine restored rooms, houses several museums.

Shopping

Milan is said to be the world's design capital, and a visit to its sensational fashion district is high on many visitors' itineraries, especially as designer clothes can cost less here than in New York or London.

The Golden Quad

Milan's most popular shopping area for *haute couture* is without doubt the network of pretty streets known as the Golden Quad, bordered by Via Montenapoleone, Via Manzoni, Via Sant'Andrea and Via Spiga. Here you will find designer clothes, accessories, shoes and leatherwear presented in chic, minimalist interiors that are works of art themselves. Even when the shops are closed, the streets are full of visitors admiring the window displays.

Other Options

You can also shop for superior goods at the glass-domed Galleria Vittorio Emanuele II (▷ 48); the bohemian Corso di Porta Ticinese, where there are smaller, trendy boutiques; or the up-and-coming Isola area, with some interesting boutiques. There are plenty of less elite stores selling more affordable items around Corso Vittorio Emanuele II, Via Torino, Corsa di Porta Romana and Corso Buenos Aires.

Interior Design Excellence

Milan is also at the forefront of interior design, ranging from the elegant to the wacky. Large

Shopping is the number one pleasure in Milan, be it for the latest designer creation, tomatoes on the vine, or gadgets and gifts

FACTORY OUTLETS

If you are unable to pay the high prices of Milan's fashion district, don't despair. Factory outlets, stores that offer last season's products at a fraction of the price, are becoming very popular in Milan. Although, as the city has a reputation to uphold as one of the world's most important fashion hubs, many of the biggest designers are reluctant to put their name to outlet stores because they don't wish to be seen selling their creations at discount prices. You can also pick up sensational bargains during the end-of-season sales (January/February or July/August).

ultramodern showrooms stocked with original trendsetting items are apparent throughout the city. Smaller items that can easily be taken home include kitchen gadgets, decorated glass and sleek, stylish lighting.

Traditional Gifts

If you are looking for more traditionally Milanese products to take home, try some *panettone* (▷ panel below) or pick up a bottle of fine Italian wine from a reputable *enoteche*, where every purchase is beautifully wrapped and you can usually sample before you buy. For that special gift, head to one of the delightful stationery shops that stock hand-crafted paper-based products. The items are produced using luxury paper, handmade from such materials as silk, coconut, lace and bamboo, in every color and shade. They will need to be carefully packed for the journey home.

Antiques Heaven

Antiques enthusiasts will enjoy browsing in the numerous antiques shops around the Brera district and along the canals, where regular antiques markets (▷ 90) are held. Shops specializing in old and new prints and lithographs, art galleries and auction houses are plentiful in Milan. For book lovers, the city has more than its fair share of spacious well-stocked bookshops, some selling books in many languages. There are also smaller, specialist bookshops that stock rare or out-of-print books.

PANETTONE

This famous Milanese cake, made with eggs, flour, sugar, candied fruits and spices, is now served at Christmas throughout Italy. It is said to have originated in the 15th century when the dessert at the Christmas Eve banquet for Ludovico Sforza was burned. It was rescued by Toni, a kitchen boy, who salvaged the remains of the burned cake and added new ingredients. Since that day 'pan del Toni' became known as *panettone* and has remained popular ever since.

Shopping by Theme

Whether you're looking for a department store, a quirky boutique, or something in between, you'll find it all in Milan. On this page shops are listed by theme. For a more detailed write-up, see the individual listings in Milan by Area.

ACCESSORIES

Alan Journo (▷ 35)
Andrew's Ties (▷ 57)
Borsalino (▷ 57)
Buccellati (▷ 35)
Bvlgari (▷ 35)
Cartier (▷ 36)
Damiani (▷ 36)
Kalos (▷ 90)
Tiffany & Co (▷ 37)

ART AND ANTIQUES

Antichità Caiati (▷ 35)
Carlo Orsi (▷ 35)
Mercato d'Antiquariato
    di Brera (▷ 76)
Old English Furniture
    (▷ 76)

BOOKS AND MUSIC

Buscemi Dischi (▷ 76)
Discovery (▷ 57)
Feltrinelli International
    (▷ 36)
Libreria Hoepli (▷ 57)
Ricordi Megastore
    (▷ 58)

DEPARTMENT STORES

10 Corso Como (▷ 76)
Coin (▷ 57)
La Rinascente (▷ 57)

FASHION

Alexander McQueen
    (▷ 35)
Anna Fabriano (▷ 90)
Armani Casa (▷ 35)
Atribu (▷ 76)
B-Fly (▷ 90)
Biffi (▷ 90)
Bottega Veneta (▷ 35)
Custo (▷ 90)
Dolce & Gabbana (▷ 36)
(ethic) (▷ 90)
Fendi (▷ 36)
Jil Sander (▷ 37)
Krizia (▷ 37)
Laura Biagiotti (▷ 37)
Liu.Jo (▷ 57)
Luisa Beccaria (▷ 76)
Mila Schön (▷ 37)
Miu Miu (▷ 37)
La Perla (▷ 37)
Prada (▷ 58)
Sisley (▷ 58)

FOOD AND DRINK

Armandola (▷ 35)
Drogheria Parini (▷ 36)
Giovanni Galli (▷ 57)
La Fungheria (▷ 76)
N'Ombra de Vin (▷ 37)
Peck Stopanni (▷ 57)

HOME AND DESIGN

Alessi (▷ 57)
Armani Casa (▷ 35)
Artemide (▷ 35)
De Driade (▷ 36)
De Padova (▷ 36)
Flos (▷ 36)
Vetrerie di Empoli (▷ 37)

LEATHER AND SHOES

Fratelli Rossetti (▷ 36)
Furla (▷ 57)
Giorgio Fedon 1919
    (▷ 90)
Salvatore Ferragamo
    (▷ 37)
Sermoneta (▷ 37)

PAMPERING

Acqua di Parma (▷ 35)
Diego della Palma
    (▷ 76)
for pets only (▷ 57)

STATIONERY

Cartoleria Ruffini (▷ 76)
E.E. Ercolessi (▷ 76)

Milan by Night

After-hours entertainment in cosmopolitan Milan is vibrant; the city is known for Italy's hippest nightlife. For the energetic, there are glitzy nightclubs, trendy bars, disco-pubs, lively cafés and live music venues. If you prefer a slower pace, the city offers world-class opera, ballet and a theater season that is the best and most varied in Italy.

What's Hot
Things don't get going until after dark, when Milan's partygoers come out to play and the streets are thronged with beautiful people. Evenings usually begin slowly, with the *passeggiata*, where everyone struts up and down the central streets, mainly around Galleria Vittorio Emanuele II and the pedestrian zones along Via Dante. As the pace picks up, three popular areas to visit are the Navigli, bisected by waterways and dotted with *osterie* and jazz bars, the atmospheric Brera district, with intimate cafés and restaurants, and the top end of Corso Garibaldi leading to the lively and trendy Corso Como.

A Little Culture
Opera fans will want to attend a performance at La Scala, Milan's famous opera house. The season runs from December to July, but performances sell out fast. There are many other places to enjoy classical music in the city, as well as live theater, cultural events and a wide repertoire of plays. The city's many cinemas often show the new releases ahead of other Italian cities.

*Opera and all that jazz—
you can find it all in Milan,
with great music venues
and places just for a drink*

DISCO-PUBS

Milan has a breed of pub popular with those who want to dance without being plunged into the noise and flashing lights of a full-blown disco; these are known as disco-pubs. Disco-pubs are ideal if you prefer to start the evening with a relaxing drink and quiet conversation, slowly building up to a party mood. Later into the evening the volume is turned up and the pub really starts to swing as every available space is taken up by disco divas performing the latest dance moves.

Eating Out

Eating is definitely one of life's pleasures in Milan. The diversity of Italy is as apparent in its food as it is in its culture and landscape. Whether you're after restaurants specializing in food from all over Italy or in international cooking, Milan can cater to all taste buds.

Meals and Mealtimes

Many working Milanese eat breakfast in a bar (a cappuccino and a sweet pastry). The day starts early, so if you are heading for breakfast in a bar, most open for business around 7–7.30. Hotels usually serve a buffet breakfast complete with fruit juice, cereal, cold meats and cheeses, which normally starts at 8, or earlier in business hotels. Lunch and dinner comprise *antipasto* (starter), *il primo* (pasta, risotto or soup), *secondo* (fish or meat) with *contorni* (vegetables) on the side, and *dolci* (dessert) or cheese. There's no pressure to wade through the whole menu; it's quite acceptable to order just one or two courses.

Where to Eat

Trattorie/osterie are usually family-run, serving simple authentic cooking and open for lunch and in the evening. But nowadays the name *osteria* is being adopted by smarter, trendy restaurants (▷ 92 panel). *Ristoranti* are more trendy and are not always open for lunch. *Pizzerie* (▷ 59 panel) specialize in pizzas, but often serve simple pasta dishes as well. Some establishments still try to add a cover charge, which includes bread, and a service charge to the bill.

Bars serve hot and cold drinks, alcohol and snacks throughout the day. It's customary to eat or drink standing up; you will pay extra to sit down. Make your request and pay at the cash desk, then take the receipt and go to the bar where you will be served. *Távole calde* are stand-up snack bars that serve freshly prepared hot food. *Gelaterie* (▷ 40) sell a range of ice cream, served in a cone or tub. The best ice cream is made on the premises.

Eat in style—Milan is a great place for dining alfresco, for coffee, lunch or a delectable ice cream

There are restaurants to suit all tastes and budgets in Milan. On this page they are listed by cuisine. For a more detailed description of each restaurant, see Milan by Area.

CAFÉS/BARS

Biffi (▷ 78)
Bindi (▷ 78)
Caffè Mercanti (▷ 59)
Caffè Victor Hugo (▷ 59)
California Bakery (▷ 92)
Camparino in Galleria
    (▷ 59)
Cova (▷ 39)
Emporio Armani (▷ 39)
Marchesi (▷ 60)
Sant'Ambroeus (▷ 60)
Victoria Caffè (▷ 60)

ELEGANT/TRENDY

Le 5 Terre (▷ 39)
Alice's Restaurant (▷ 78)
L'Amour (▷ 39)
Aimo e Nadia (▷ 105)
Atlas Foyer (▷ 105)
Bice (▷ 39)
Bvlgari (▷ 39)
Il Giorno Bistrot (▷ 106)
Just Cavalli Café (▷ 78)
Santini (▷ 40)
Savini (▷ 60)
Sophia's (▷ 78)

FISH/VEGETARIAN

Asso di Fiori (▷ 105)
La Cozzeria (▷ 106)
Da Gaspare (▷ 105)
Joia (▷ 39)
L'Olandese Volante
    (▷ 106)

ICE CREAM

La Bottega del Gelato
    (▷ 105)
Il Gabbiano (▷ 60)
Orsi (▷ 106)
Schockolat (▷ 78)

INTERNATIONAL

Kazan (▷ 92)
Langosteria 10 (▷ 92)
Nobu (▷ 40)
Rangoli (▷ 40)
Warsá 71 (▷ 40)
Yar (▷ 60)

MILANESE/ITALIAN

Acquasala (▷ 105)
Al Mercante (▷ 59)
Amici del Liberty (▷ 92)
Boeucc (▷ 59)
Cantina della Vetra
    (▷ 92)
Cracco (▷ 59)
Dal Bolognese (▷ 39)
El Brellín (▷ 106)
La Latteria (▷ 40)
L'Osteria di Brera (▷ 78)
Ristorante Sant'Eustorgio
    (▷ 92)
Rocking Horse (▷ 78)
La Tavernetta da Elio
    (▷ 40)
Solferino (▷ 40)

PIZZERIE

Agnello (▷ 59)
Be Bop (▷ 105)
Charleston (▷ 59)
Di Gennaro (▷ 60)
Transatlantico (▷ 40)

TRATTORIE/OSTERIE

Al Pont de Ferr (▷ 105)
C'Era Una Volta (▷ 78)
Il Giardinetto (▷ 92)
Osteria dei Binari (▷ 92)
Ponte Rosso (▷ 106)
Il Solito Posto (▷ 106)
Trattoria All'Antica (▷ 92)
Trattoria Milanese (▷ 60)
Trattoria Tre Torre
    (▷ 106)
Le Vigne (▷ 106)

Top Tips For...

However you'd like to spend your time in Milan, these top suggestions should help you tailor your ideal visit. Each sight or listing has a fuller write-up elsewhere in the book.

CUTTING-EDGE DESIGN

Cruise the Quadrilatero d'Oro (▷ 28–29) to see window displays presenting designers' creations straight off the catwalk.

Step inside shops like Dolce & Gabbana (▷ 36) on Via della Spiga and be amazed by the innovative interior designs.

Eat at Roberto Cavalli's steel-and-glass restaurant (▷ 78), decked out in his own pioneering designs.

Bring your home into the 21st century with a trendsetting item from De Driade (▷ 36).

ESCAPING THE HEAT AND NOISE

Lose yourself among the vast lawns and parkland of Parco Sempione (▷ 70).

If you really want to escape the city, head for Lake Como (▷ 101), only an hour away by train.

Take a diversion around the corner from Milan's exclusive shopping area to Giardini Pubblici (▷ 24).

Wander along the towpath of the canals (▷ 96) and find an *osteria* for lunch.

A GOOD NIGHT OUT

La Scala (▷ 58) is a must for a night to remember; book well in advance.

Have a meal and catch a late-night showing at the Cinema Odeon 5 (▷ 58).

Start the evening early by joining 'happy hour' (▷ 91), or with a cocktail at Jamaica (▷ 77) then on to Hollywood (▷ 77) till the early hours.

Join the football-crazy Milanese to see AC or Inter play at the San Siro (▷ 103); discuss the game afterward over a drink at Bar Magenta (▷ 77).

Up-to-the-minute window displays in Milan (above)

A stroll in the park (above); visit to the opera (right)

Plenty of choices on the menus in Milan (below)

A TASTE OF TRADITION

Fraternize with the locals at Trattoria Milanese (▷ 60); nearly a century of tradition is crammed into this homey restaurant.
Sample a taste of old Milan under beamed ceilings or on the shady terrace at El Brellín (▷ 106).
For excellent food that lives up to the Milanese tradition try Solferino (▷ 40).
La Latteria (▷ 40) is one of the best examples of good regional cooking in Milan.

YOUR COFFEE IN STYLE

You won't be able to resist Biffi's (▷ 78) mouthwatering chocolate cake.
Cova (▷ 39) is a great place to rest your weary feet from the perils of excessive shopping.
Enjoy people-watching with your cappuccino at Camparino in Galleria (▷ 59).
Take your pit-stop at the Emporio Armani Caffè (▷ 39) if you want to see and be seen—it's one of the most fashionable spots in town.

THE DOLCE VITA

Join an elite clientele for some luxurious pampering at Principe di Savoia (▷ 112).
Book one of the rooms with chromotherapy, aromatherapy and Japanese massage chaise longues at the Straf (▷ 112).
Indulge yourself in sumptuous surroundings haunted by royals and celebrities at the Grand Hotel de Milan (▷ 112).
Stay at the opulent Four Seasons hotel (▷ 112) in a 14th-century monastery set around a cloistered courtyard.

Stylish eating is the order of the day (above)

Elaborate oriental decoration on the table (left)

HOME-GROWN DESIGNERS

A stylish designer suit; fun and games at a kids' workshop (below)

Visit at least one of Giorgio Armani's stores (▷ 35, panel), scattered throughout the Quad.

There's a Dolce & Gabbana (▷ 36) around every street corner.

Treat yourself at Roberto Cavalli (▷ 37, panel), then flaunt your purchase at Just Cavalli Café (▷ 78).

Spoil your feet after all that walking; Salvatore Ferragamo (▷ 37) has just the thing.

FUN WITH THE KIDS

Learn about creatures from under the water at the art nouveau Acquario (▷ 74).

Try the hands-on exhibits at the Science and Technology Museum (▷ 84–85).

Allow the kids to let off steam in Parco Sempione (▷ 70), and then have a picnic.

Sit on swivelling seats and gaze at the stars in the Planetarium (▷ 24).

IF FUNDS ARE SHORT

Visit the city's free museums, which include Museo di Milano (▷ 32).

Save up to 25 percent at one of Milan's designer factory outlets (▷ 10, panel).

If you're likely to use public transport, buy a travel card (▷ 118), it's cheaper.

Consider staying at Hotel Due Giardini (▷ 109) for good value for money.

Take a tram to the Brera (above) and then go dancing (below)

SOMEWHERE TO DANCE

Rub shoulders with celebs at Tocqueville 13 (▷ 77).

The bank vaults come alive at Le Banque (▷ 58).

Drop in on one of Old Fashion Café's (▷ 77) theme nights.

Try your hand at Latin-American dancing at Tropicana Club Latino (▷ 104).

Milan by Area

PRA

The northeast reflects the diverse nature of Milan. At its heart are the chic designer shops for which the city is so famous. Alongside are elegant *palazzi*, interesting museums and a tranquil park.

2
3
4
5
6
Consiglio
BASTIONI DI PORTA NUOVA
VIALE MONTE SANTO
Fatebene-fratelli
Via Milazzo
Via Marsala
Solferino
Via San Marco
Via Castelfidardo
Nuova
Via Fatebenesorelle
Porto
Via A G Appiani
Parini
P
Repubblic
TURATI
Via
Via
della
Piazza S Angelo
Moscova
Donegani / Moscova
S Bart
Int d Finanza
Via
Marco
Via San Fermo
Piazza C Mirabello
di
S Angelo
Largo G Donegani
F
Donegani / Moscova
Via
Montebello
Turati
Via Ancona
San
Via Goito
Via Cernaia
Corso
Chiesa Prot
Via Carlo Porta
VIA
D
P
San Marco
Piazza San Marco
VIA
Questura
Via M De Marchi
Teatro
FATEBENEFRATELLI
Cavour
Piazza Cavour
Via Fiori Oscuri
Museo del Risorgimento
Via dell' Annunciata
Archi di Porta Nuova
Palazzo di Brera
P
Palazzo Borromeo
Manzoni
Palazzo dell' Informazione
Pinacoteca di Brera
Via
Borgonuovo
Piazza S Erasmo
Pisoni
Teatro Manzoni
VIA
P
Orto Botanico
QUADRILATERO D'ORO
P
Croce Rossa
Via Fratelli Cabba
Montenapoleone
Via Borgospesso
Gesu
della
Monte di Pietà
Pieta
Alessandro
Via
Via S Spirito
Museo Bagatti Valsecchi
Monte
di
Andegari
Via
Bigli
Montenapoleone
Via Monte
P
Via S Andrea
Via
Museo Poldi Pezzoli
Napoleone
Museo di Milano
Via Pagu
Via G Morone
P
0   250 m
0   250 yds
G
H

Repubblica
Repubblica
BASTIONI DI PORTA VENEZIA
Via A Manuzio
Via A Zarotto
Via Lazzaretto
Viale
Via
Vittorio
Veneto
Vitt Veneto
Lazzaretto
Via L Palazzi
Via Lecco
Via A Tadino
Via P
Via Castaldi
Via
CORSO BUENOS AIRES
Via A Cadamosto
Manin
Giardino
zoologico
Museo del
cinema
Giardini
Pubblici
Palazzo
Dugnani
Bastioni di
Porta Venezia
Porta Venezia
Oberdan
Piazza
G Oberdan
Liberty-Style
Architecture
Planetario
VIALE PIAVE
VIALE LUIGI MAJNO
Museo
di Storia
Naturale
Via
Palestro
Palazzo
centro
svizzero
Villa
Belgiojoso
Bonaparte
VENEZIA
Vecchio Politecnico
Marina
ACI
Palestro
Palazzo Rocca
Saporiti
Palestro
Piazza
E Duse
Palestro
Via
Via Boschetti
CORSO
Via G Serbelloni
Via
Cappuccini
Via Vivaio
Via
Palazzo
del Senato
Via S Primo
SENATO
Spiga
Palazzo
Serbelloni
Mozart
Istituto
dei Ciechi
Via
VIA S DAMIANO
Palazzo
Arcivescovile
Prefettura
S Babila
J
K

Giardini Pubblici

TOP 25

Take your pick— summer rides in the Giardini Pubblici make a welcome change

THE BASICS

- ✠ J3
- ✉ Corso Venezia, Via Manin, Via Palestro
- ◷ 6.30am–dusk
- 🍴 Café/bar
- Ⓜ Turati, Palestro, Porta Venezia, Repubblica
- 🚌 61, 94; tram 1, 2, 29, 30
- ♿ Good
- ✋ Free

Planetarium
- ✠ K4
- ✉ Corso Venezia 57, 20121
- ☎ 02 8846 3340
- ◷ Shows Sep–Jun Tue, Thu 9pm, Sat–Sun 3, 4.30pm; Jul–Aug times vary (see monthly schedule)
- Ⓜ Palestrol
- 🚌 Tram 9, 29, 30
- ♿ Good
- ✋ Moderate

HIGHLIGHTS

- Museo di Storia Naturale (▷ 33)
- Planetarium

The largest gardens in Milan were created on the lines of an English park. The attractions and summer entertainment, set among vast greenery and vibrant blooms, are a real breath of fresh air for adults and children alike.

Peace and tranquility The public gardens extend for about 160,000sq m (192,000sq yards) and were designed by Giuseppe Piermarini in 1786. They were enlarged in 1857 by Giuseppe Balzaretto to include the Palazzo Dugnani and the Villa Belgiojoso Bonaparte (▷ 30–31). Further changes were made by Emilio Alemagna for the International Expo of 1871, incorporating waterfalls and fountains. Nowadays the gardens provide a welcome escape from the city heat and noise, and attract many joggers and family picnickers. In summer donkey rides, minitrain rides and a merry-go-round keep children amused for hours.

Not just a park There's something here for all ages and interests, from rocks and minerals to bugs. Life-sized crocodiles and snakes seem almost real. On the east side of the park is the Museo di Storia Naturale (▷ 33), popular for its reconstructed dinosaur collection.

View the stars Next to the natural history museum is the Planetario Ulrico Hoepli. The Planetarium was built in 1930 and is the biggest in Italy. It has a huge domed room where projections take place. Themes change monthly—call or check details at the tourist office.

Museo Bagatti Valsecchi

Stunning blue-and-white patterned floor at the Museo Bagatti Valsecchi

This charming museum, in a neo-Renaissance palace, houses fascinating antiques and curios and an extraordinary collection of genuine and reproduction furnishings of the brothers Fausto and Giuseppe Bagatti Valsecchi.

Ardent collectors Fausto and Giuseppe Bagatti Valsecchi, born respectively in 1843 and 1845, inherited their artistic flair from their father, a famous miniaturist. Using a large team of Lombard artisans, they skillfully renovated two *palazzi* (one in Via Gesù, the other backing onto it in Via Santo Spirito) between 1876 and 1895, to be used as their own home. Descendants of the brothers lived here until 1974 and created the Fondazione Bagatti Valsecchi, to open the collection to the public.

Genuine or reproduction? You can visit the brothers' private apartments and the formal rooms they shared: the drawing room, hall of arms, dining room, study and Santo Spirito atrium. The Renaissance setting can be quite convincing—as can be the reproduction furniture that is integrated with the authentic pieces. The Camera Rossa has a charming display of 15th- to 17th-century children's furniture, while the dining room contains tapestries, sideboards and kitchenware. The library has a number of valuable 15th-century parchments. In the Valtellinese bedroom there is a wonderful 16th-century bed with carved scenes of *The Road to Calvary* and the Old Testament, together with paintings by Giampietrino.

Museo Poldi Pezzoli

TOP 25

The Gondola on the Lagoon *by Francesco Guardi (1712–93), in the Museo Poldi Pezzoli*

THE BASICS

www.museopoldipezzoli.it

✚ H5

✉ Via Manzoni 12, 20121

☎ 02 794 889

🕐 Tue–Sun 10–6. Closed 1 Jan, 6 Jan, Easter, 25 Apr, 1 May, 1 and 15 Aug, 1 Nov, 8 Dec, 25 and 26 Dec

Ⓜ Montenapoleone

🚌 61, 94; tram 1, 2

♿ Access to elevator on request

✋ Expensive

ℹ Audiotours, shop

HIGHLIGHTS

In the Salone Dorato:
- *Portrait of a Young Woman*, Piero del Pollaiolo—this lovely portrait has become a symbol of the palace
- *The Virgin and the Child*, Sandro Botticelli
- *St. Nicholas of Tolentino*, Piero della Francesca
- *Madonna and Child*, Andrea Mantegna
- Arms collection

The palace and its exquisite collection of paintings and decorative arts belonged to Gian Giacomo Poldi Pezzoli, a 19th-century Milanese aristocrat. Each room was planned to evoke a style of the past.

Stunning collection With the considerable fortune inherited from both sides of the family, Poldi Pezzoli (1822–79) amassed a large collection of antiques and art, the nucleus of which was his remarkable armory. With the advice of leading experts, Poldi Pezzoli built up a collection of armor, furniture, textiles, ceramics, bronzes and *objets d'art*. Pride of place, however, goes to his fabulous collection of paintings. On his death, he left the palace and its contents "to the use and benefit of the public". The building was badly bombed in 1943, but was rebuilt, retaining the original decoration where possible. Through gifts and bequests, the museum considerably enlarged its collection in the 1970s and 1980s.

Art and arms The two floors of exhibits are connected by a charming staircase with landscape paintings and a black marble fountain. The ground-floor rooms are devoted to the Armory, in its stunning neo-Gothic setting, the Fresco Room, the textile collections and library. The main collections are upstairs: paintings from the 14th- to 16th-century Lombard School, northern Italian works of art from the 14th to 18th centuries and the Salone Dorato, or Golden Room, which is full of Renaissance masterpieces. Further rooms display jewelry, sundials, clocks and watches.

Pinacoteca di Brera

The Brera gallery offers the chance to see one of the finest collections of northern Italian paintings. From small beginnings, it was enlarged by Napoleon to include works by the region's major artists.

Impressive collection The gallery is in the Palazzo Brera, a baroque palace built on the site of a 14th-century Jesuit convent. Empress Maria Theresa of Austria evicted the Jesuits, redesigned the palace in neoclassical style and founded the Accademia di Belle Arti in 1773. The Pinacoteca opened in 1809, showing mostly works that had been confiscated by Napoleon from churches and convents in French-occupied territories: Lombardy, Veneto, Emilia-Romagna and the Marche. Through donations and exchanges, the collection has been growing ever since. In 1882, the Accademia di Belle Arti and the Pinacoteca became independent, and the gallery became a state-owned art museum.

An art lover's heaven The works of art are arranged in 38 large rooms, making for pleasant viewing. Although the collection spans six centuries and includes some non-Italian artists (El Greco, Anthony Van Dyck, Rubens, Rembrandt), the emphasis is on northern Italian 15th- to 16th-century art. The collection is full of gems by the leading Renaissance masters, with the Venetian collection the largest and most important outside Venice. Here, too, you have a chance to study the Lombard masters of the Renaissance. The two most famous paintings in the collection are by Piero della Francesca and Raphael.

THE BASICS

www.brera.beniculturali.it

G4

Via Brera 28, 20121

02 9280 0361

Tue–Thu, Sat–Sun 8.30–7.15. Fri 8.30am–9.15pm. Closed 1 Jan, 1 May, 25 Dec

Lanza, Montenapoleone

61; tram 1, 4, 12, 14, 27

Good, elevator

Moderate

Audiotours in English, book and souvenir shop

HIGHLIGHTS

- Jesi Collection—paintings and sculpture from the first half of the 19th century
- *Marriage of the Virgin* (1504), Raphael
- *Montefeltro Altarpiece* (1472–74), Piero della Francesca
- *Dead Christ*, Mantegna
- Portraits by Lotto, Tintoretto, Titian
- *Virgin of the Rose Garden*, Bernardino Luini
- *The Kiss*, Francesco Hayez

Quadrilatero d'Oro

HIGHLIGHTS

● Cova at Via Montenapoleone 8 (▷ 39), a historic café with tantalizing window displays of patisserie, sweets and chocolates. Sip coffee at the bar or sit in one of the smart salons with well-dressed Milanese
● One of the best spots in Europe to window shop
● Aristocratic residences

TIP

● Make an early start to avoid the crowds, but most shops won't open before 9.30am.

Milan is Italy's high spot for fashion and the area known as the Quadrilatero d'Oro (The Golden Quad) is the most exclusive shopping quarter in the city. Whatever fashion designer you are looking for, you will find them here.

Glitz and glamor The Quadrilatero d'Oro is defined by Via Montenapoleone, Via Manzoni, Via della Spiga and Via Sant'Andrea. Via Manzoni is wide and traffic laden, the other streets in the shopping quarter are relatively quiet and make for pleasant shopping and give the opportunity just to window-shop. Via Montenapoleone, familiarly known as Montenapo, is the most famous of these exclusive streets, flaunting world-famous designer names such as Ferragamo, Armani, Valentino, Prada and Versace, and high-class jewelers.

Palaces, courtyards and museums The name Quadrilatero d'Oro comes from the early 19th century and the quarter still preserves some of its historic *palazzi* as well as many fascinating court-yards. Via Bigli has the oldest buildings, with some of the palaces dating back to the 17th century. The shopping district is also home to the Museo Bagatti Valsecchi (▷ 25) and two civic museums, both at Via Sant'Andrea 6: the Museo di Milano (▷ 32) and the Museo di Storia Contemporanea (Contemporary History).

Milan style Don't expect a bargain unless you come during the January sales; the prices here tend to be higher than the rest of the city. The window fronts are stylish, artfully displaying the latest trends in fashion, as well as showcasing jewelry, fine leather, luxury furs and accessories.

THE BASICS

✚ H4

✉ 20121

🕐 Varied. Most shops close on Sun and Mon, though some are open on Mon afternoon. Most open at 9am or 9.30am

🍴 Numerous, with some very chic ones

Ⓜ San Babila, Montenapoleone

🚌 61, 94; tram 1, 2

♿ Good

Villa Belgiojoso Bonaparte

HIGHLIGHTS

● Marino Marini Collection
● Museo dell'Ottocento
● *Quarto Stato* (Fourth Estate): Pelizza da Volpedo depicts the struggles and sufferings of the working classes
● Lovely wooded gardens

TIP

● Choose a sunny, or at least dry, day to visit the villa and its gardens. You will be close to the Giardini Pubblici for a walk or picnic afterward.

This vast neoclassical villa has been occupied by Napoleon and Josephine, Count Joseph Radetzky (the Austrian commander-in-chief) and the Italian royal family. Part is now home to the Museo dell'Ottocento (19th-Century Museum).

Famous residents The villa was built in 1790 by Leopold Pollack for Count Ludovico Barbiano di Belgiojoso. After the count's death in the early 19th century, the Italian government donated it as a residence for Napoleon and Josephine, and it passed into the hands of the city of Milan in 1921.

Milanese collectors Occupying 35 rooms, the Museo dell'Ottocento illustrates the main artistic movements of the 19th and early 20th century, with emphasis on Italian and French

Il Quarto Stato (The Fourth Estate) by Guiseppe Pellizza da Polpedo, depicting the workers' march; the painting is displayed in the Museo dell'Ottocento, which is located in the Villa Belgiojoso Bonaparte, on the edge of Giardini Pubblici

art. The rooms cover art from the neoclassical period to Romanticism, from the Scapiglliatura (a Milan-based movement) through Divisionism to Realism. The three most important collections are the Grassi, Vismara and Marino. The Marino Marini Collection opened in 1973 and contains bronzes, portrait busts and drawings by the Italian sculptor Marini (1901–80). Some of the busts depict the artist's friends and acquaintances (among them Ivor Stravinsky, Henry Miller, Henry Moore and Marc Chagall) and are remarkable for their psychological insight.

Beyond the walls The small building beside the villa is the Padiglione d'Arte Contemporanea (PAC), which hosts temporary modern art exhibitions. There are good views of the English-style gardens from the upper floors of the villa.

THE BASICS

www.villabelgiojosobona parte.it

✚ J4

✉ Via Palestro 16, 20121

☎ 02 7634 0809

🕓 Tue–Sun 9–1, 2–5.30 (last admission 5)

Ⓜ Palestro

🚌 61, 94; tram 1, 2

♿ Good

✋ Free

More to See

ARCHI DI PORTA NUOVA
This large, double-arched gateway separates Via Manzoni and Piazza Cavour. This and Porta Ticinese are the only surviving gates of the medieval walls that protected the city.
✛ H4 ✉ North end of Via Manzoni, 20121 Ⓜ Montenapoleone 🚌 61, 94; tram 1, 2

BASTIONI DI PORTA VENEZIA
On the site of one of the Porte Regie (Royal Gates) in the Spanish city walls, constructed in the 16th century, the present-day arch dates from 1828.
✛ K3 ✉ Piazza Oberdan, 20129 Ⓜ Porta Venezia 🚌 Tram 9, 29, 30

LIBERTY-STYLE ARCHITECTURE
Streets around Piazza Oberdan make up one of Milan's best neighborhoods for Liberty-style architecture, known outside Italy as art nouveau. Two good examples are on Via Malpighi, Nos. 3 and 12, and another is at Via Frisi 2, known as Palazzina Liberty. Heading south from Piazza Oberdan on Viale Piave, look for floral motifs at No. 42, one of Milan's best Liberty buildings, and also notice No. 11, the Casa Bossi, with its elaborate balconies.
✛ K4 ✉ Around Piazza Oberdan, 20129 Ⓜ Porta Venezia 🚌 Tram 9, 29, 30

MUSEO DEL RISORGIMENTO
www.museodelrisorgimento.mi.it
This museum is in the neoclassical Palazzo Moriggia and traces Italy's history from Napoleon's campaigns in Italy (1796 and 1800) to Unification in 1866. Exhibits include prints and paintings, original documents, busts, mementoes and proclamations. You can see the first Italian flag (Primo Tricolore), which was used at the Battle of Arcole Bridge in 1796.
✛ H4 ✉ Via Borgonuovo 23, 20121 ☎ 02 8846 4117 🕐 Tue–Sun 9–1, 2–5 Ⓜ Montenapoleone 🚌 41, 61; tram 1, 2 ♿ Good ✋ Moderate, free on Fri after 2

MUSEO DI MILANO
www.museodistoriacontemporanea.it
Together with the Museo di Storia Contemporanea, an exhibition space for modern history and lectures, the Museo di Milano is located in the

Roman tombstones from the first century AD in the Archi di Porta Nuova

Deer statues outside the Natural History Museum

Palazzo Morando Attendolo Bolognini. The rooms of the 18th-century palace display the original furniture and decor and recall a typical noble family's residence. On show are paintings, prints and objects from the 18th century until the end of the 19th century.

✚ J5 ✉ Via Sant'Andrea 6, 20121 ☎ 02 8846 5933 🕓 Tue–Sun 2–5.30 🚇 Montenapoleone 🚌 61, 94; tram 1, 2 ♿ Good ✋ Free

MUSEO DI STORIA NATURALE

www.comunemilano.it/museostorianaturale

Occupying 23 rooms of a huge mock-Romanesque late-19th-century building on the edge of the Giardini Pubblici, this museum has sections on geology, mineralogy, palaeontology, entomology, zoology and habitats. Children will love the dinosaurs and the life-size reproductions of crocodiles, snakes and sea creatures. Explanations in Italian only.

✚ K4 ✉ Corso Venezia 55, 20121 ☎ 02 8846 3337 🕓 Tue–Sun 9–5.30 🚇 Palestro 🚌 Tram 9, 30 ♿ Good ✋ Moderate, free on Tue after 2, daily after 4.30

PALAZZO SERBELLONI

www.fondazioneserbelloni.com

This monumental neoclassical palace has played host to famous figures such as Napoleon and Josephine and Vittorio Emanuele II. It was built in 1793, and was partially restored after bombings in World War II. During office hours, you can walk through the huge arched entrance to the frescoed loggia and arcaded courtyard.

✚ J5 ✉ Corso Venezia 16, 20121 ☎ 02 7600 7687 🚇 San Babila 🚌 61

SAN MARCO

Built in 1254, the present church was founded on the site of the 12th-century church of San Marco. It was designed in Romanesque style, but underwent major Gothic and baroque transformations—plus 19th-century restoration. The main portal, with bas-reliefs, and the tower, with decorative friezes (only seen from Via Pontaccio), survive from the 13th-century church.

✚ G4 ✉ Piazza San Marco 2, 20121 ☎ 02 2900 2598 🕓 Daily 7.30–1, 4–7.15 🚌 61, 43 ♿ Good (chapels have steps) ✋ Free

Detail of the first vault in the presbytery of San Marco

From Retail to Calm

Window-shop in Milan's bustling fashion quarter and then take a well-earned rest in the public gardens.

DISTANCE: 3.2km (2 miles) **ALLOW:** Half a day to include shopping and sights

START

VIA MONTENAPOLEONE
✚ H5 🚇 Montenapoleone

END

GARDINI PUBBLICI
✚ J3 🚇 Porta Venezia/Palestro

❶ Walk down Via Montenapoleone from where it joins Via Manzoni, one of the best spots to window-shop in Europe, overflowing with top designer names and excellent coffee stops.

❷ As you go, explore the smaller streets to the left of Via Montenapoleone. At the end of Via Montenapoleone turn left and then left again into Corso Venezia.

❸ Take the next left into Via della Spiga for more exclusive shops. Half-way down, cross over Via Sant'Andrea, home to the Museo di Milano (▷ 32).

❹ Continue past Via Gesù on the left, and then Via Santo Spirito, also on the left, where you can detour to the Museo Bagatti Valsecchi (▷ 25), with its superb interior furnishings.

❺ Continue on Via della Spiga to the end of the street and turn right.

❻ Pass under the Archi di Porta Nuova (▷ 32) into Piazza Cavour. Keep to the right side and take the 2nd right into Via Palestro. About halfway along here is the Villa Belgiojoso Bonaparte (▷ 30–31).

❼ The villa houses the Museo dell'Ottocento (Museum of the 19th Century) and is set in an English garden. Cross over the road and enter the Giardini Pubblici (▷ 24). Inside the park is the Museum of Natural History (▷ 33).

❽ Another attraction here is the Planetarium (▷ 24) in the far eastern corner. You can exit near here for the Porta Venezia metro.

ACQUA DI PARMA

www.acquadiparma.com
Items to pamper the feet, body, face and scalp, and leather pouches in which to put your new purchases.
✚ J5 ✉ 3 Via Gesù, 20121 ☎ 02 7602 3307 Ⓜ Montenapoleone

ALAN JOURNO

www.alanjourno.com
Crazy bags, hats and lots more in eccentric styles displayed around a stainless steel and glass staircase that spirals over three levels.
✚ J4 ✉ Via della Spiga 36, 20121 ☎ 02 7600 1309 Ⓜ Montenapoleone

ALEXANDER MCQUEEN

www.alexandermcqueen.com
This store reveals a series of interconnecting rooms to show off the designer's unique styles.
✚ H5 ✉ Via Pietro Verri 8, 20121 ☎ 02 7600 3374 Ⓜ Montenapoleone

ANTICHITÀ CAIATI

www.caiati.it
Exclusive gallery specializing in Venetian landscapes and 17th- and 18th-century Italian paintings.
✚ J5 ✉ Via Gesú 17, 20121 ☎ 02 794 866 Ⓜ Montenapoleone

ARMANDOLA

An elegant deli that reflects its exclusive location in its prices. But the tempting aroma of cheese and the display of freshly made pastas and jars of truffles make it worth every cent.
✚ J4 ✉ Via Borgospresso 21, 20121 ☎ 02 7602 1657 Ⓜ Montenapoleone

ARMANI CASA

www.armanicasa.com
Yet another one for the Armani empire. No longer just fashion, Armani is synonomous with a whole lifestyle. Sophisticated, stylish furniture and lovely accessories for the home.
✚ H4 ✉ Via Manzoni 37, 20121 ☎ 02 657 2401 Ⓜ Montenapoleone

ARTEMIDE

www.artemide.com
Renowned for forthright modern designs for the home, created by top designers, the products are displayed to best effect in a gallery-like showroom.
✚ J5 ✉ Corso Monforte 19, 20122 ☎ 02 7600 6930 Ⓜ San Babila

BOTTEGA VENETA

www.bottegaveneta.com
The well-known name in Italian fashion opened this immense "maison" branch in 2013 as a second sales point to its flagship store on Via Montenapoleone. It carries the entire range, from leather goods to clothing and furniture, in an 18th-century *palazzo*.
✚ J5 ✉ Via Sant'Andrea 15, 20121 ☎ 02 7787 8116 Ⓜ San Babila

BUCCELLATI

www.mariobucellati.it
Unique bespoke jewelry featuring an extraordinary collection of silver animals.
✚ J4 ✉ Via Montenapoleone 23, 20121 ☎ 02 7600 2154 Ⓜ Montenapoleone

BVLGARI

www.bulgari.com
The Milan branch of the world-famous fashion jeweler and watchmaker.
✚ J5 ✉ Via Montenapoleone 2, 20121 ☎ 02 777 001 Ⓜ San Babila

CARLO ORSI

www.galleriaorsi.com
The paintings, bronze sculpture, furniture and precious stones sold here are a collector's dream.
✚ J5 ✉ Via Bagutta 14, 20121 ☎ 02 7600 2214 Ⓜ San Babila

EMPIRE OF ARMANI

Milan-born designer Giorgio Armani began his career as a window dresser at the city's La Rinascente department store, and in 1961 progressed to the menswear shop Nino Cerruti. In 1975, Armani branched out alone, and within 10 years had become a household name when he revolutionized the industry with his more wearable and less-expensive collection. The Armani Empire took another giant leap forward in 2000, when it opened its flagship store, Emporio Armani, in Milan (✉ Via Manzoni 31, 2021 ☎ 02 7231 8600; www.emporioarmani.it).

CARTIER
www.cartier.com
Police-guarded Cartier has gold, silver and porcelain that is the stuff of dreams, as are the prices.
✚ H5 ✉ Corner Via Montenapoleone and Via Gesù 2, 20121 ☎ 02 3030 0421 Ⓜ San Babila

DAMIANI
www.damiani.it
Damiani have been creating bold designs using high-quality gems since 1924. Also classy watches, strings of pearls and fine wedding rings.
✚ J5 ✉ Via Montenapoleone 10, 20121 ☎ 02 7602 8088 Ⓜ San Babila

DE DRIADE
www.driade.it
Founded in 1968, De Driade is always seeking new trends in home and office furniture, with some items going on to become collectors' items.
✚ H4 ✉ Via Manzoni 30, 20121 ☎ 02 7631 3860 Ⓜ Montenapoleone

DE PADOVA
www.depadova.it
Elegance and simplicity are key at this shop for the discerning homeowner. Only the finest materials are used.
✚ J5 ✉ Corso Venezia 14, 20121 ☎ 02 777 201 Ⓜ San Babila, Palestro

DOLCE & GABBANA
www.dolcegabbana.it
At the cutting edge of fashion and straight off the catwalk, this amazing store is worth a look for the decor alone.
✚ J4 ✉ Via della Spiga 26 20121 ☎ 02 795 747 Ⓜ Montenapoleone

DROGHERIA PARINI
Upstairs for mouthwatering confectionery and downstairs to the arched cellar for wines and spirits, organic jams and jellies, compotes and chutneys, and excellent blends of coffee and tea—all beautifully gift-wrapped. Very friendly and helpful staff.
✚ H4 ✉ Via Borgospesso 1, 20121 ☎ 02 3668 3500 Ⓜ Montenapoleone

FELTRINELLI INTERNATIONAL
www.lafeltrinelli.it
This branch of the famous bookstore is where the world's fashion hierarchy come to buy their British and American *Vogues*, *Elles* and *Cosmopolitans*. Good selection of travel books, too.
✚ H4 ✉ Piazza Cavour 2, 20122 ☎ 02 659 5644 Ⓜ Turati

FENDI
www.fendi.com
Edoardo Fendi and his wife founded a small leatherware shop in Rome in 1925; their five daughters went on to develop it into a powerful fashion, perfume and accessories empire.
✚ J5 ✉ Via Montenapoleone, 20121 ☎ 02 7602 1617 Ⓜ San Babila

FLOS
www.flos.com
High-quality ultramodern lighting for the home and office, with contemporary creations by names such as Philippe Starck and Jasper Morrison.
✚ J5 ✉ Corso Monforte 9, 20122 ☎ 02 798 457 Ⓜ San Babila

FRATELLI ROSSETTI
www.rossetti.it
This family company, founded 30 years ago by the brothers Renzo and Renato, pushes Salvatore Ferragamo (▷ 37) for the title of Italy's best shoe store, and has slightly lower prices than its rival.
✚ J5 ✉ Via Montenapoleone 1, 20121 ☎ 02 7602 1650 Ⓜ San Babila

JIL SANDER

www.jilsander.com
Avant-garde cuts and attention to detail are the trademarks of this famous German designer. Styles for both men and women.
H5　Via Pietro Verri 6, 20121　02 777 2991　San Babila

KRIZIA

Lower in the fashion firmament than Armani or Versace, but Krizia has a high profile in Italy, especially for knitwear.
J5　Via della Spiga 23, 20121　02 7600 8429　San Babila

LAURA BIAGIOTTI

www.laurabiagiotti.it
Easy-to-wear fashion, gentle on the eye and less aggressively "high fashion" than some designers.
H4　Via Borgospesso 19, 20121　02 799 659　Montenapoleone

MILA SCHÖN

www.milaschon.com
Known for elegant interchangeable separates that are typical of Milanese trends.
H4　Via Manzoni 45, 20121　02 0265 3354　Montenapoleone

MIU MIU

www.miumiu.com
Urban chic from the House of Prada. Check out the high-tech interior.
J5　Via Sant'Andrea 21, 20121　02 7600 1799　San Babila

N'OMBRA DE VIN

www.nombradevin.it
This shop has a fine collection of wines from Italy, France and the New World. You can taste before you make your decision to buy.
G4　Via San Marco 2, 20121　02 659 9650　Turati, Moscova

LA PERLA

www.laperla.it
Sultry and sophisticated underwear and swimwear, made in the finest fabrics.
J5　Via Montenapoleone 1, 20121　02 7600 0460　San Babila

SALVATORE FERRAGAMO

www.salvatoreferragamo.it
Italy's most famous shoe

designer, whose stores grace exclusive shopping streets all over the world.
J5　Via Montenapoleone 3, 20121　02 7600 0054　San Babila

SERMONETA

www.sermonetagloves.com
Handmade leather gloves in every size, shade and style you can imagine.
J5　Via della Spiga 46, 20121　02 7631 8303　San Babila

SHOWROOM 43 VIA MANZONI

www.43viamanzoni.it
Showing exclusively collections made in Italy, such as Valentini, Marol, Dalmini and Italo Ferretti, Showroom 43 provides a one-stop shop for menswear classics.
H4　Via Manzoni 43, 20121　348 510 9747　Montenapoleone

TIFFANY & CO

www.tiffany.com
Legendary jewelers selling crystals, gold and silverware, clocks and jewelry, at prices designed for the super-rich.
J5　Via della Spiga 19a, 20121　02 7602 2321　San Babila

VETRERIE DI EMPOLI

www.vetreriediempoli.it
Gorgeous hand-decorated glasses, chandeliers, vases and fruit dishes.
J4　Via Montenapoleone 22, 20121　02 7600 8791　Montenapoleone

Entertainment and Nightlife

ANTEO

www.spaziocinema.info
One of Milan's leading original-language cinemas, with an emphasis on art house. Films from countries such as Sweden, Japan or France are often shown with English subtitles.

✛ G4 ✉ Via Milazzo 9, 20121 ☎ 02 597 7732 🚇 Moscova

DIANA MAJESTIC BAR

Partake of sophisticated cocktails and aperitifs in the bar at the Sheraton Diana Majestic hotel (▷ 112). Sit out in the elegant gardens during summer, while the lavish lounge and opulent bar are a great pit-stop in the cooler months.

✛ K4 ✉ Viale Piave 42, 20129 ☎ 02 2058 2004 🚇 Porta Venezia

THE FRIENDS

www.thefriendsmilano.it
This is where to go if you are feeling nostalgic for a British pub; the building was even sent in parts from England. Lots of Victoriana decor and all the beers and lagers you should want.

✛ J3 ✉ Viale Monte Santo 12, 20124 ☎ 02 2900 5315 🚇 Repubblica

LELEPHANTE

www.lelephant.com
One of the city's leading hangouts for dressed-up partyers and trendy students. Decked out with innovative plastic furniture. Aimed at both the straight and gay crowd.

✛ L4 ✉ Via Melzo 22, 20129 ☎ 02 2951 8768 🚇 Porta Venezia

PISCINA COZZI

Located on the tree-lined Via Tunisia just north of the Giardini Pubblici, this swimming pool complex has two pools, one of which is Olympic size with 5m (16ft) and 10m (33ft) diving boards. It can get crowded in high season but it is the closest place in central Milan to cool off. Open every day but check in advance for session times.

TICKET INFORMATION

Tickets for plays and concerts can be booked through agencies and also from specialist booking offices such as the Ricordi Box Office in Galleria Vittorio Emanuele II (☎ 02 7200 7031), or Fnac at Via Torino on the corner with Via Palla (www.fnacitalia.it ☎ 02 878 004) and Box Ticket Free Shop in the Stazione Centrale (☎ 02 669 6757). Tickets for La Scala (▷ 58) need to be purchased well in advance—it may be possible on very rare occasions to get a ticket two hours before a performance. Tickets can be purchased from a ticket office in the Duomo metro station or online. (Scala Infotel Service www.teatroalla scala.org ☎ 02 7200 3744.)

✛ K3 ✉ Via Tunisia 35, 20124 ☎ 02 659 9703 🚇 Porta Venezia, Repubblica

TEATRO MANZONI

www.teatromanzoni.it
This theater is particularly popular with the Milanese and produces a variety of performances, including serious drama such as plays by Chekhov and Brecht, Italian plays, one-person shows, stand-up comedy, classical music concerts and musicals; come on Sunday morning for jazz.

✛ H4 ✉ Via Manzoni 42, 20121 ☎ 02 763 6901 🚇 Montenapoleone

TEATRO SAN BABILA

www.teatrosanbabilamilano.it
Tradition is the key here, and the Milanese flock to see famous actors and directors stage their best-loved works of drama in this 500-seat performance venue. Be sure to reserve well in advance.

✛ J5 ✉ Corso Venezia 2/a, 20121 ☎ 02 798 010 🚇 San Babila

THAT'S AMORE

www.thatsamore.it
One of Milan's most respected bars, attracting fashionable drinkers of all ages. Sip your cocktails at the sleek, curvy silver bar. Early aperitifs may descend into dance floor revelry before the night is over.

✛ J3 ✉ Viale Monte Santo 8, 20124 ☎ 02 2906 0626 🚇 Repubblica

PRICES

Prices are approximate, based on a 3-course meal for one person.

€€€   over €50
€€   €20–€50
€   under €20

LE 5 TERRE (€€–€€€)

www.ristorantele5terre.com
In business for more than 20 years, this restaurant is the master of Ligurian cuisine, particularly renowned for fish dishes, athough carnivores are catered to. Leave room for the delicious desserts. The surroundings are elegant and the excellent wine list comprehensive.
✚ H3   ✉ Via Andrea Appiani 9, 20121   ☎ 02 657 5177   ◷ Daily lunch, dinner. Closed evenings Nov–Dec   Ⓜ Repubblica, Turati

L'AMOUR (€€)

www.lamour.it
The perfect place for after-show dinner in classic surroundings with an up-to-date twist and subtle lighting. Fish or meat mains and tasty desserts.
✚ G3   ✉ Via Solferino 25, 20121   ☎ 02 659 0176   ◷ Tue–Sun lunch, dinner. Closed Aug   Ⓜ Moscova

BICE (€€)

www.bicemilano.it
Founded in 1926, Bice is on one of the smartest streets in the fashion district. Extensive à la carte menu; lighter set menu for lunch.

✚ H4   ✉ Via Borgospesso 12, 20121   ☎ 02 7600 2572   ◷ Mon–Sat lunch, dinner   Ⓜ Montenapoleone

BVLGARI (€€€)

www.bulgarihotels.com
Mix with the seriously rich crowd at this smart restaurant in the Bvlgari hotel on the edge of the Orto Botanico. Gorgeous terrace and gardens.
✚ H4   ✉ Via Fratelli Gabba 7b, 20121   ☎ 02 805 8051   ◷ Daily lunch, dinner   Ⓜ Montenapoleone

COVA (€€)

www.pasticceriacova.com
In business since 1817, this landmark café is an ideal stop for a break from shopping. It is expensive but the coffee and cakes are irresistible.

ANYONE FOR COFFEE?

The Milanese have coffees to suit different types of food or to be drunk at different times of day. Cappuccino, or the longer and milkier *caffè latte*, are often the choice at breakfast, followed by *espresso* for a short kick-start of caffeine later in the day. Not many visitors will risk the *ristretto*, as this is the strongest of them all. Cappuccino is never drunk by Italians after lunch or dinner. Other varieties are *caffè americano* (full cup and watery), *caffè freddo* (iced coffee) and *caffè macchiato* (*espresso* "stained" with a dash of milk).

✚ H5   ✉ Via Montenapoleone 8, 20121   ☎ 02 7600 0578   ◷ Mon–Sat all day   Ⓜ San Babila, Montenapoleone

DAL BOLOGNESE (€€€)

www.dalbolognese.it
Packed with a glitzy Milanese crowd—fashion and media folk and football players. The food is strictly Bolognese: homemade pastas, meats and great desserts. Eat outside in the fine weather.
✚ J3   ✉ Via Amedei 8, 20123   ☎ 02 6269 4845   ◷ Closed Sat lunch and Sun   Ⓜ Repubblica

EMPORIO ARMANI CAFFÈ (€€)

www.armaniristorante.com
Why not take a break for a designer coffee, pastries, light lunches, juices or a cocktail after browsing this sleek store, the flagship of the famous designer.
✚ H4   ✉ Piazza Croce Rossa 2, 20121   ☎ 02 6231 2680   ◷ Mon–Sat all day   Ⓜ Montenapoleone

JOIA (€€€)

www.joia.it
Closeness to nature is the philosophy behind this first-class vegetarian restaurant, where the freshest of ingredients are lovingly prepared to tempt the palate.
✚ K3   ✉ Via P. Castaldi 18, 20124   ☎ 02 2952 2124   ◷ Mon–Sat lunch, dinner. Closed 3 weeks Aug   Ⓜ Repubblica, Porta Venezia

LA LATTERIA (€–€€)

Busy family-run restaurant serving food from the Lombardy region. Haunt of journalists and the occasional celebrity in search of home cooking.
✚ G3 ✉ Via San Marco 24, 20121 ☎ 02 659 7653 ● Mon–Fri lunch, dinner 🚇 Moscova

NOBU (€€€)

www.noburestaurants.com
Chef Nobuyuki Matsuhisa has been creating culinary treats for more than 10 years in the Armani store. Japanese cuisine meets South American and Californian influences. Very smart and very expensive.
✚ H4 ✉ Via Alessandro Manzoni 31, 20121 ☎ 02 7231 8645 ● Mon–Sat lunch, dinner; Sun dinner only 🚇 Montenapoleone

RANGOLI (€)

www.rangoli.it.
Authentic North Indian cuisine in the Brera district. The dishes cooked in the *tandoor* (clay oven) are particularly popular. There is a good vegetarian menu.
✚ G3 ✉ Via Solferino 36, 20121 ☎ 02 2900 5333 ● Tue–Fri lunch, dinner; Sat–Mon dinner only 🚇 Moscova

SANTINI (€€€)

www.santinirestaurant.com
This is the epitome of sophistication with cool, clean lines and modern lighting. The striking blue-and-white dining room is very distinctive. A full menu features fusion and Piedmont cuisine, or try light lunch options such as spaghetti or vegetable wraps. Alternatively you can opt for the special "Taste of Santini" menu featuring the chef's specials. There's a covered garden for alfresco eating.
✚ G3 ✉ Via San Marco 3, 20121 ☎ 02 655 5587 ● Mon–Fri lunch, dinner; Sat lunch only 🚇 Lanza

SOLFERINO (€€)

www.ilsolferino.com
One of the oldest restaurants in the city, which serves excellent Milanese dishes in beautiful surroundings. Meat and fish dishes are to the fore, but there are also good choices for vegetarians.
✚ H3 ✉ Via Castelfidardo 2, 20121 ☎ 02 2900 5748 ● Daily lunch, dinner 🚇 Moscova

ITALIAN ICE CREAM

The Italians justifiably pride themselves on their superior ice cream, and Milan regards itself as one of the best ice-cream-making areas in the country. There are *gelaterie* dating back to the mid-19th century that are still in business; some have as many as 100 different varieties on offer. Many make their ice cream with all natural ingredients and you often find a wonderful array of fresh fruits to accompany your choice.

LA TAVERNETTA DA ELIO (€€)

www.tavernetta.it
In the same family since 1957, this restaurant is preferred by celebrities and literary types. The cuisine is Tuscan in its most traditional forms— thick soups, pastas and hearty meat dishes. Tuscan wines and good desserts.
✚ H4 ✉ Via Fatebenefratelli 30, 20121 ☎ 02 653 441 ● Mon–Fri lunch, dinner; Sat dinner only 🚇 Montenapoleone, San Babila

TRANSATLANTICO (€)

Delicious pizza in this well-known art nouveau pizzeria. Try one of the unusual combinations, such as pizza stuffed with mussels and squid.
✚ K3 ✉ Via Malpighi Marcello 3, 20129 ☎ 02 2952 6098 ● Wed–Mon 🚇 Porta Venezia

WARSÁ 71 (€€)

www.ristorantewarsa.it
Ethiopian restaurant decorated in authentic African style. The main course is designed to be shared between two people: spiced meat and vegetables served on a thin, spongy bread called *ingerà*, which is used instead of cutlery. Finish off with tea with cinnamon and cloves.
✚ K3 ✉ Via Melzo 16, 20129 ☎ 02 201 673 ● Thu–Tue lunch, dinner 🚇 Porta Venezia

Here is the heart of historic Milan and the meeting place for tourists and locals alike. The Piazza Duomo is dominated by the splendid wedding-cake of a cathedral, the third-largest in the world.

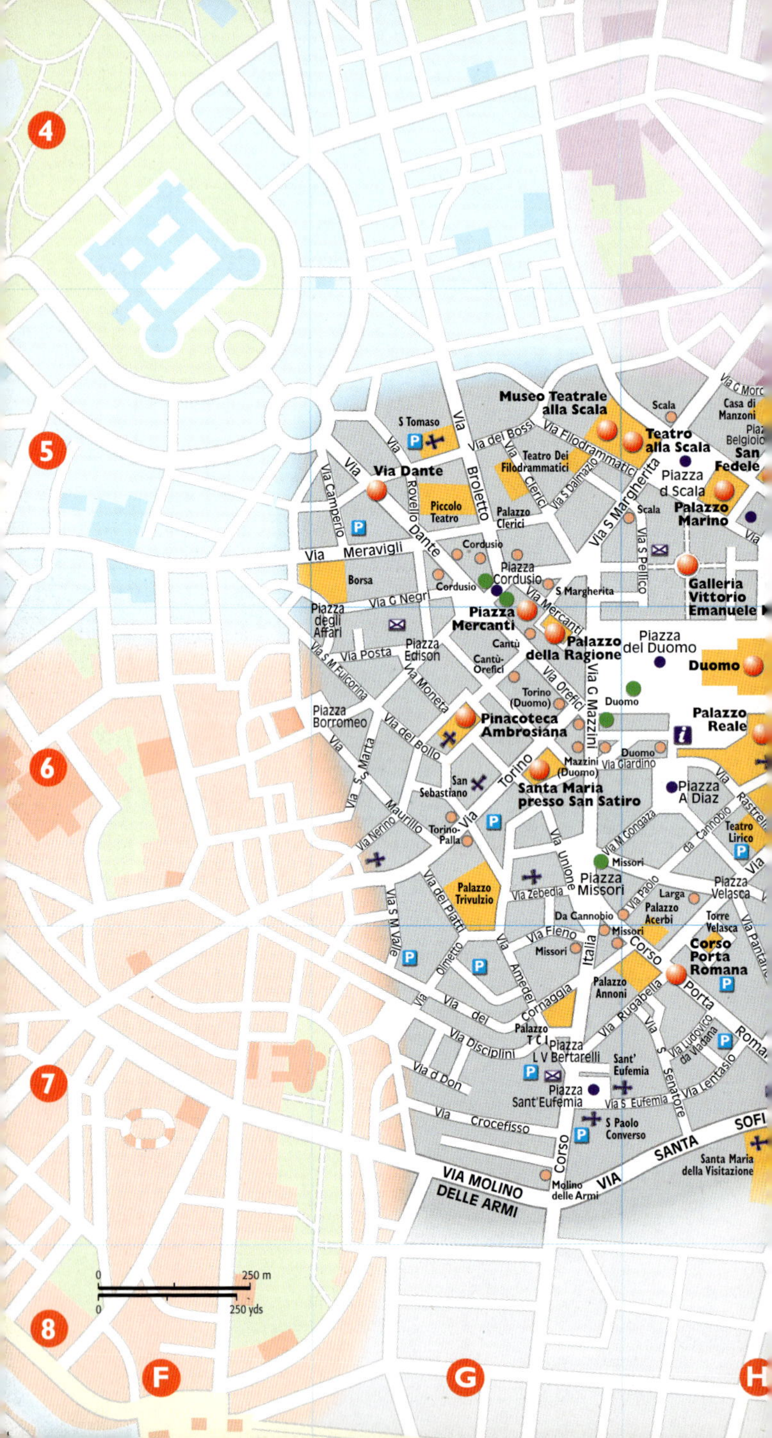

4
5
6
7
8
F
G
H
Museo Teatrale alla Scala
Scala
Casa di Manzoni
Piazz Belgioio
S Tomaso
Via del Bossi
Via Filodrammatici
Teatro alla Scala
San Fedele
Via
Via Dante
Teatro Dei Filodrammatici
Via S Margherita
Via Clerici
Piazza d Scala
Scala
Broletto
Via S Dalmazio
Via Camperio
Piccolo Teatro
Palazzo Clerici
Palazzo Marino
Rovello
Via
Cordusio
Piazza Cordusio
Via S Pellico
Galleria Vittorio Emanuele
Via Meravigli
Dante
Borsa
Cordusio
S Margherita
Via G Negri
Via Mercanti
Piazza degli Affari
Piazza Mercanti
Piazza del Duomo
Piazza Edison
Cantù
Palazzo della Ragione
Duomo
Via S M Fulcorina
Via Posta
Cantù-Orefici
Via G Mazzini
Via Oreci
Via S Marta
Via Moneta
Torino (Duomo)
Duomo
Piazza Borromeo
Via del Bollo
Pinacoteca Ambrosiana
Duomo
Palazzo Reale
Via Giardino
Via
San Sebastiano
Torino
Mazzini (Duomo)
Piazza A Diaz
Rastren
Via Nerino
Torino-Palla
Santa Maria presso San Satiro
Teatro Lirico
Via
Via Unione
Via M Congaza
da Cannobio
Via
Missori
Palazzo Trivulzio
Via Zebedia
Piazza Missori
Via Paolo
Larga
Piazza Velasca
Via del Piatti
Da Cannobio
Palazzo Acerbi
Torre Velasca
Via S M Vale
Via Fieno
Missori
Italia
Corso
Corso Porta Romana
olmetto
Missori
Palazzo Annoni
Via Rugabella
Via
Porta
Via Amedei
Palazzo
Via ludovico da Viadana
Romana
Via dei
Cornaggia
T C I
Piazza L V Bertarelli
Sant' Eufemia
Via Lentasio
Via Disciplini
Via d'Don
Piazza Sant'Eufemia
Via S Eufemia
Via Senatore
SANTA SOFI
Via Crocefisso
S Paolo Converso
Santa Maria della Visitazione
Corso
VIA MOLINO DELLE ARMI
Molino delle Armi
VIA
SANTA
0   250 m
0   250 yds

Centro Storico
Palazzo Belgioioso
Museo Manzoniano
Via M A Catena
Corso G Matteotti
Corso Monforte
Via Agnello
Teatro Nuovo
Piazza S Babila
Via S Pietro all'Orto
Piazza Liberty
S Babila
Padegonda
Corso Vittorio Emanuele II
Largo A Toscanini
Via Borgogna
Via P Mascagni
Corso Europa
Via Durini
VIA VISCONTI DI MODRONE
S Vito
Palazzo Durini
Cerva
Via C Beccaria
Palazzo del Capitano di Guistizia
Via
Piazza Fontana
Piazza Fontana
Largo dei Bersaglieri
Largo Augusto
Palazzo Arcivescovile
Augusto
SFORZA
Larga Verziere
Via d'signora
Sforza
Palazzo Reale
Piazza S Stefano
Largo
Palazzo Sormani (Biblioteca)
Ufficio Comunale
S Stefano Maggiore
Via Bergamini
FRANCESCO
Via P Andreani
Antonio
Università degli Studi di Milano
Chiaravalle S
Perdono
Giardino Guastalla
Via Festa d
Ca'Granda
Via San Barnaba
Largo F Richini
S M Annunciata
VIA
San Nazario Maggiore
San Nazaro in Brolo
S Sofia
J
K

Ca' Granda

HIGHLIGHTS

● Cortile Maggiore—the spacious and elegant main courtyard with arcades surrounding the garden

● Fine 15th-century facade

This huge building certainly lives up to its name—Casa Grande or Large House. It houses the Humanities Department of the State University and retains elegant 15th-century courtyards and the lovely baroque Cortile Maggiore (Great Court).

Milan's benefactor Otherwise known as the Ospedale Maggiore, the building was commissioned by Francesco Sforza in the mid-15th century as the main hospital in Milan, which it remained for nearly five centuries. The plans of his architect, Filarete, were based on a rectangle made up of 10 equal squares with a church in the middle. Although Filarete's designs defined the entire building, only the right wing was constructed under the Sforzas. Guiniforte Solari (1429–91) completed Filarete's Renaissance section with the upper floor

in Gothic style. In 1624, Francesco Maria Richini enlarged the hospital, and in 1797 the left wing was added. Ca' Granda was badly damaged by bombing in 1943, and owes its present-day look to postwar reconstruction and restoration, when it was converted to house the university.

Elegant but practical The lengthy facade (282m/925ft) illustrates the different stages of construction from the 15th century (on the far right) through to the late 18th century. The main courtyard is the Cortile Maggiore, with the Basilica dell'Annunciata opposite the entrance, and to the right are other elegant 15th-century courtyards. The hospital was very progressive for its day: men and women were separated, sanitary services were in corridors, and the beds had built-in cupboards and folding tables.

THE BASICS

- ✚ H7
- ✉ Via Festa del Perdono 5, 20122
- ☎ 02 503 111
- 🕐 Mon–Fri 8–6, Sat 8–12.30. Closed Aug
- 🍴 Basic student canteen
- Ⓜ Missori
- 🚌 54, 77, 94; tram 12, 16, 23, 24, 27
- ♿ Good
- ✋ Free
- ℹ No information or booklets

Duomo

HIGHLIGHTS

- The roof and the view
- The apse
- Stained-glass windows
- Trivulzio Candelabra (12th-century, crafted in gold)
- Treasury's collection of gold and silverwork
- The elaborate crypt

TIP

- Be prepared for some scaffolding on the cathedral due to ongoing restoration work. Most of the major work is now complete.

Symbol of the city, the sumptuous Duomo, with its huge proportions, towers over the Piazza Duomo. An ascent to the roof reveals a wonderful panorama of Milan and beyond.

Dazzling and ethereal The Duomo bristles with Gothic statues, gargoyles, pinnacles and soaring spires and has attracted comments from the censorious "an imitation hedgehog" (D.H. Lawrence) to the lyrical "a poem of marble" (Mark Twain). Ascend to the roof, by steps or elevator, for a wonderful panorama of Milan and, on a clear day, a view as far as the Alps.

Controversial building Milan's Duomo was founded in 1386 under the ambitious Gian Galeazzo Visconti, who resolved to build the

Clockwise from far left: soaring skyward—the elaborate towers of Milan's extraordinary cathedral; the structure dominates Piazza Duomo; feeding the pigeons in the piazza; detail of the intricate stonework; exquisite ornamentation inside; a singing angel sculpture adorns the facade

THE BASICS

www.duomomilano.it

✚ H6

✉ Piazza del Duomo, 20121

☎ 02 7202 3375

🕐 Cathedral daily 7–6.30. Baptistery San Giovanni Alle Fonti 10–6; closed 1 Jan, 1 May, 15 Aug, 25 Dec. Terraces 9–6. Baptistery of San Stefano daily 9–7; closed 1 May, 25 Dec (enter North lift)

🚇 Duomo

🚌 Tram 1, 2, 3, 15, 24 and others

♿ Main cathedral good. Crypt and Treasury none

✋ Cathedral free (fee for photography). S Giovanni moderate; terraces expensive; S Stefano free

biggest church in Italy. Although the church was consecrated in 1418, it remained incomplete for more than four centuries. Work finally started on the facade in the early 17th century, but was only finished in 1812, under Napoleon.

Into the darkness The Duomo is 157m (515ft) long, 33m (108ft) wide across the nave and 92m (302ft) wide across the transept; the roof is decorated with 2,245 statues, 135 spires and 96 gargoyles; the interior can hold 40,000 people. It is topped by the Madonnina, (the little Madonna), a gilded copper statue hoisted up here in 1774. After the stunning white exterior, the interior feels gloomy, but in the darkness your eye is drawn to the lively stained-glass windows. Monuments include the extraordinary statue of *The Flayed San Bartolomeo* (1562), with his skin draped over his shoulders.

Galleria Vittorio Emanuele II

The Galleria is perfect for a stroll, to window-shop or pause for a sophisticated break

THE BASICS

✠ H5

✉ Galleria Vittorio Emanuele II, 20121

☎ 02 7740 4343

🕓 Most shops daily 9am–10pm; some close 2–4

🍴 Plenty (▷ Highlights, below)

🚇 Duomo

🚌 61; tram 1, 2, 3, 14, 15, 24

♿ Good

HIGHLIGHTS

● Watching the fashionable Milanese
● Savini restaurant (▷ 60)
● Camparino in Galleria—have a cocktail or a coffee in the famous period café (▷ 59)
● Excellent boutique shopping

Linking Piazza del Duomo and Piazza della Scala, this elegant glass-roofed arcade has long been a popular rendez-vous for the Milanese. It's worth indulging in a pricey cappuccino to watch the perpetual parade of stylish locals.

City reconstruction It was in 1865, after Unification, that the architect Giuseppe Mengoni offered his silver trowel to King Vittorio Emanuele II —after whom the arcade was named—to lay the foundation stone of the Galleria. Sadly, Mengoni fell to his death from the scaffolding a few days before the inauguration in 1897. The project's completion, in 1898, was marked by building a triumphal arch at the Duomo end. The creation of the arcade and the colossal demolition process that it involved reshaped the whole structure of the city.

Glitzy Milan This is a great place for shopping, eating and drinking—if you can afford it. The glass roof gives the arcade a feeling of light and space, even on a dull day. There are excellent bookshops, music stores and leather and clothes boutiques. A focal point is the central octagon area, under the glass dome, 47m (154ft) high. Pavement mosaics depict the coats of arms of the Savoy family and the symbols of Italian cities: Milan (red cross on a white background), Turin (a bull), Florence (a lily) and Rome (a she-wolf). Milanese tradition has it that stepping on the genitalia of the bull will bring you good luck. Savini (▷ 60), one of Milan's finest restaurants, is traditionally the meeting place of opera fans after first nights at La Scala.

The exterior of the Palazzo Reale, where banners advertise the temporary exhibitions

Palazzo Reale

In the heart of the city, beside (and inevitably dwarfed by) the Duomo, this historic palace was seat of the city council in the 11th century, ducal residence of the Viscontis and Sforzas, and the royal palace of the Austrian rulers.

A plethora of museums The palazzo has been rebuilt several times, the present-day building owing its neoclassical appearance to the 1770s redevelopment of the square. It is worth a visit to see several beautifully restored rooms, and the Museo della Reggia, the pre-1990 works from the Civico Museo d'Arte Contemporanea (CIMAC) Contemporary Art collection, and for the major topical art exhibitions that are held here.

History of art The 11th-century Palazzo Broletto Vecchio (Courthouse) was rebuilt by the ruling Viscontis between 1330 and 1336, and redesigned in the 16th century by the Sforzas. Mozart performed at the hall here in 1770, when he was 14. In the following decade the palace was rebuilt by Giuseppe Piermarini. Large sections of the palace were demolished in the 1920s and 1930s, and most of its dazzling interior was destroyed in the bombings of 1943. In the 1960s, the city bought the palace for use as museums, offices and to display art exhibitions. CIMAC was housed here in 1983, but has now closed and its fine collection of paintings with works by Picasso and Matisse has moved to Villa Belgiojoso (▷ 30–31). The Museo del Duomo, next to the Palazzo Reale, charts the history of the cathedral and was reopened in 2013.

THE BASICS

✚ H6
✉ Piazza del Duomo 12, 20122
☎ 02 860 165
🕐 Palazzo Reale: Mon 2.30–7.30, Tue–Wed, Fri 9.30–7.30, Thu, Sat, 9.30am–10.30pm. Museo della Reggia: Tue–Sun 9.30–7.30. Museo del Duomo Tue–Sun 10–6. Closed 1 Jan, 1 May, 15 Aug, 25 Dec
🚇 Duomo
🚌 54; tram 1, 2, 3, 12, 14, 15, 16, 19, 23, 24, 27
♿ Good
✋ Palazzo Reale expensive. Museo della Reggia free. Museo del Duomo moderate
ℹ Palazzo Reale bookshop for temporary exhibitions only

HIGHLIGHTS

● Museo della Reggia
● Restored apartments
● Films and concerts in the palace courtyards in summer

Piazza Mercanti

Locals and visitors alike gather at the attractive Piazza Mercanti

THE BASICS

- ✚ G6
- ✉ Piazza Mercanti, 20123
- Ⓜ Duomo
- 🚌 Tram 2, 3, 14, 15, 24
- 🍴 Al Mercante (café with outdoor tables, ▷ 59)

HIGHLIGHTS

- Loggia degli Orsi
- Palazzo delle Scuole Palatine (1645), a baroque palace with sculptures of St. Augustine and the Latin poet Ausonius
- Palazzo Panigarola, a handsome building with Gothic ogee arches

For centuries the administrative and commercial hub of the city, this central market square is rich in architecture and history. Rather more intimate than most piazzas in Milan, it is traffic-free and preserves its medieval character.

Origins The first buildings in this piazza were established in the 13th century and the square was enclosed by six gates, accessible only to the citizens of the quarter. The Palazzo della Ragione, built between 1228 and 1233 (▷ 54), served as the city's law courts over five centuries, and its loggia was used for medieval market stalls.

Intimate appeal The piazza used to be much bigger, stretching to the far side of the present-day Via Mercanti, the wide pedestrian thorough-fare. On the north side is the huge Palazzo dei Giureconsulti, which houses the Chamber of Commerce. The Loggia degli Orsi, facing the Palazzo della Ragione, is a lovely pink-and-gray marble building that immediately draws the eye. The ground-floor arcade, now a bank, was used as a market. The coats of arms above are those of patrician families who lived in the quarter. Today, the piazza is a popular rendezvous, a pleasant spot for browsing in *bouquinistes* or lunching alfresco. The central well, with two Ionic columns supporting a pediment, dates from the 16th century. Unlike the nearby Piazza del Duomo, which is large and impersonal, the Piazza Mercanti has retained its intimate charm and even McDonald's at the east end manages to keep a low profile.

Pinacoteca Ambrosiana

Cardinal Federico Borromeo built the Palazzo Ambrosiana in 1608 to house his collection of books and manuscripts. The art collection includes outstanding works by 15th- and 16th-century Italian and Flemish masters.

Phenomenal collection In the early 17th century, Cardinal Federico Borromeo commissioned eight experts to travel through Europe and the Middle East to amass a collection for his library. The Biblioteca Ambrosiana was set up with around 30,000 prints and 14,000 manuscripts. Nine years later, his personal collection of 127 paintings was added to form the Pinacoteca Ambrosiana. The building was extended in the 19th century, and today is run by a private and autonomous ecclesiastical foundation. From 1990 to 1997 the gallery closed for radical restructure; 10 new rooms were made accessible, enabling around 400 paintings to be displayed. Works by Leonardo, Titian, Raphael and Caravaggio are among those exhibited.

Essential viewing The ground-floor library has more than 1,000 pages of drawings by Leonardo da Vinci—only accessible to scholars. On the first floor, rooms 1 and 4–7 display the Borromeo collection: Tuscan, Lombard and Venetian Renaissance and 17th-century Flemish art. The drawings displayed under glass are Leonardo reproductions. Rooms 2 and 3 display Renaissance masterpieces. Rooms 8–24 have 14th- to 20th-century paintings, sculpture and *objets d'art*, culminating in Manfredo Settala's diverse scientific collection.

Teatro alla Scala

TOP 25

Italy's premier opera house, built by Giuseppe Piermarini in the 18th century

THE BASICS

www.teatroallascala.org

✠ H5

✉ Piazza della Scala, 20121

☎ La Scala Information Point and La Scala Bookstore (Piazza della Scala 5) 02 7200 3744

🕐 Opera season opening night always 7 Dec, feast day of Sant'Ambrogio, patron saint of Milan

Ⓜ Duomo, Cordusio

🚌 61; tram 1, 2

✋ Varies for performances; museum moderate

♿ Good

DID YOU KNOW?

● The opera house has exceptionally fine acoustics.

● The stage is one of the largest in the world, measuring 1,200sq m (4,300sq ft).

● Most of the world's best-known conductors and opera singers have performed here.

● Tickets are notoriously hard to get, so book well in advance (performances sell out months in advance).

The world-famous La Scala, commissioned by Empress Maria Theresa of Austria, has seen the premières of many great classical Italian operas. The facade on Piazza della Scala is surprisingly sober, and belies the sumptuous auditorium.

World famous The opera house takes its name from the Santa Maria della Scala, the church on whose site it was built in 1776–78. It was built by Giuseppe Piermarini, architect of the Palazzo Reale, and took the place of the smaller Regio Ducale Teatro, which had been destroyed by fire. After the 1943 bombings, La Scala was the first of the city's monuments to be rebuilt. It reopened in 1946 and was re-inaugurated by Toscanini. The former artistic director came back from America after 17 years, having fled from Fascist Italy in 1929. Musical works by Rossini, Donizetti, Bellini, Verdi and Puccini had their debuts here, not always to great acclaim—the first night of Puccini's *Madame Butterfly* in 1904 was a complete fiasco—no one liked it!

Sumptuous interior The plush auditorium is decorated in red velvet and gilded stuccowork, with a 365-lamp crystal chandelier; it has an overall seating capacity of 2,015. You can view the auditorium as part of a museum tour. The Museo Teatrale alla Scala (▷ 54) contains a huge collection of theatrical memorabilia among its interesting exhibits.

Major overhaul The opera house was revamped between 2002 and 2004, when the stage was completely rebuilt and sound quality enhanced.

More to See

CORSO PORTA ROMANA

The ancient route to Rome started at the Porta Romana (Roman Gate). One of the city's busiest streets, it is lined with small shops, pastisseries and cafés. The buildings of architectural interest, neoclassical and flamboyant art nouveau *palazzi*, lie toward the Piazza Missori end.

H7 20121 Missori, Crocetta, Porta Romana 77; tram 24

MUSEO MANZONIANO

www.casadelmanzoni.mi.it

Overlooking Piazza Belgioioso in the heart of the city, this was the home of Alessandro Manzoni, considered the greatest Italian novelist of the 19th century. Born in Milan, he lived here almost continuously, from 1814 until he died in 1873. You can visit his study, library, the living rooms, the wedding bedroom and the bedroom where he died.

H5 Via G. Morone 1 (Piazza Belgioioso), 20121 02 8646 60403 Tue–Fri, Sun 9–12, 2–4 Duomo 61; tram 1, 2 Good Free

MUSEO TEATRALE ALLA SCALA

www.teatroallascala.org

The museum was founded in 1913 and has a superb collection of theatrical memorabilia. This ranges from ornate stage-curtains and antique musical instruments to costumes (including those for Maria Callas and Rudolf Nureyev) and the Sambon collection of paintings and ceramics. You can take a tour of the auditorium, too.

G5 Piazza della Scala, 20121 02 8879 7473 Daily 9–12.30, 1.30–5.30, last visit 5. Closed 1 Jan, Easter Sun, 1 May, 15 Aug, 7 Dec, 25–26 Dec Duomo, Cordusio 61, tram 1, 2 Good Moderate

PALAZZO DELLA RAGIONE

http://palazzodellaragionefotografia.it

A splendid redbrick medieval building, with rounded arches and a ground-floor loggia that dominates Piazza Mercanti (▷ 50). It was built in 1233 by the *podestà* (governor) and now hosts photographic art shows.

G6 Piazza Mercanti, 20123 Tue–Sun 9.30–8.30, Thu, Sat until 10.30pm Duomo Tram 2, 3, 15, 24

Splendid statue on the facade of the Palazzo della Ragione

PALAZZO MARINO

On the same square as the Teatro alla Scala, this is an imposing baroque palace with a late-19th-century facade. It was built in 1558 for Tommaso Marino, a wealthy Genoese financier, and since 1860 it has been the city's town hall. The palace is not open to the public, but don't miss the porticoed Courtyard of Honour, which can be glimpsed from Via Marina.

✠ H5 ✉ Piazza della Scala, 20121 ◷ View from outside only Ⓜ Duomo, Cordusio 🚌 61; tram 1, 2

SAN FEDELE

www.sanfedele.net

This church is one of the city's finest examples of baroque architecture. The elaborate facade is decorated with reliefs on the pediment and sculpted figures in the niches. Although internally less exciting, the church has some beautifully carved wooden furniture.

✠ H5 ✉ Piazza Fedele, 20121 ☎ 02 8635 2215 ◷ Mon, Wed–Thu 10–1 Ⓜ Duomo 🚌 61; tram 1, 2 ♿ Poor; 7 steps up to church ✋ Free

SANTA MARIA PRESSO SAN SATIRO

This gem of a church is squeezed between four streets southwest of the Duomo. The original ninth-century building was brilliantly restructured by Donato Bramante, who created the illusion of depth by using gilded stucco and *trompe l'oeil*.

✠ G6 ✉ Via Speronari 3, 20123, entrance on Via Torino ☎ 02 7202 1804 ◷ Mon–Sat 9.30–5.30, Sun 2–5.30 Ⓜ Duomo 🚌 Tram 2, 3, 14, 15, 16, 24 ♿ Good ✋ Free

VIA DANTE

Linking Largo Cairoli to Castello Sforzesco, this pedestrian thoroughfare was built at the end of the 19th century. Alfresco cafés spill out onto the street, and elegant shops occupy the lower floors of fine neoclassical buildings. The northwest end of the street is dominated by an equestrian statue of Garibaldi and beyond it is the soaring clock tower of the Castello.

✠ G5 ✉ 20121 Ⓜ Cordusio, Cairoli 🚌 18, 50, 58; tram 19, 24 and others

Santa Maria Presso San Satiro church

Eating alfresco on the Via Dante

City Highlights

This stroll through the heart of Milan will introduce you to some of the city's most famous landmarks.

DISTANCE: 2km (1.25 miles) **ALLOW:** 2 hours plus stops

START

PIAZZA DEL DUOMO
H6 Duomo

END

PIAZZA DEL DUOMO
H6 Duomo

1 Start at the Piazza del Duomo, dominated by the west front of the Duomo (▷ 46–47). Walk along the right side of the cathedral and turn right down the narrow Via del Palazzo Reale.

8 Passing in front of La Scala, follow Via Santa Margherita down to Piazza Mercanti (▷ 50), into Via Mercanti, which leads back to the Duomo.

2 Pass between Palazzo Reale (▷ 49) and Palazzo Arcivescovile. Go round the back of the latter via the bell tower and the rotunda. Turn left at the end of Via delle Ore.

7 Now in Piazza Belgioioso you can find Manzoni's house, now the Museo Manzoniano (▷ 54). Continue to Via Manzoni, where Museo Poldi Pezzoli (▷ 26) is on the right. Turn left back into Piazza della Scala, with the opera house, La Scala (▷ 52), on your right.

3 Enter Piazza Fontana, with the 1783 fountain by Piermarini. Look behind it for a fine view of the Duomo and then return to the Piazza del Duomo.

6 Here, too, is the statue of writer Manzoni. Leaving the piazza the way you entered, walk alongside the church. You will see Casa degli Omenoni ahead on the left, once home to the sculptor Leone Leoni.

4 Turn right through Galleria Vittorio (▷ 48) into Piazza della Scala. Cross in front of the Palazzo Marino and turn right. Take another right behind the *palazzo*.

5 This brings you into the Piazza San Fedele, with its baroque church.

ALESSI

www.alessi.com
Alessi has everything for the home and office, including drinks accessories from wine coolers to corkscrews, as well as textiles and funky items for children's rooms.
✚ J5 ✉ Corso Matteotti 9, 20121 ☎ 02 795 726 Ⓜ San Babila

ANDREW'S TIES

www.andrewsties.com
Italian ties made of wool, silk and cashmere in every imaginable shade and design. Shirts and sweaters as well.
✚ H5 ✉ Galleria Vittorio Emanuele II, 20121
☎ 02 860 935 Ⓜ Duomo

BORSALINO

www.borsalino.com
Milan's oldest milliners should be the first port of call if you are looking for a hat.
✚ H5 ✉ Galleria Vittorio Emanuele II, 20121
☎ 02 8901 5436 Ⓜ Duomo

DISCOVERY

Browse through rare vinyl albums by the Beatles, Lou Reed, Jimi Hendrix, and lots more at this record stall under the arches.
✚ G6 ✉ Passaggio Santa Margherita (just off Piazza Mercanti), 20123 ☎ 339 699 9417 Ⓜ Duomo

FOOTBALL TEAM DUOMO

Deck yourself in the colors of Milan's football favorites at the Juventus Corner, their official gear and sportswear section in this mega football fan emporium. Or pick up a shirt, flag or hat emblazoned with the national team insignia.
✚ H6 ✉ Piazza Duomo 20, 20122 ☎ 02 8905 2922 Ⓜ Duomo

FOR PETS ONLY

www.forpetsonly.it
For dogs who yearn to look every bit as chic as their owner; clothes, leads, baskets and lots more in the latest styles and fashions.
✚ G5 ✉ Via S. Pietro all'Orto 3, 20122 ☎ 02 795 694 Ⓜ San Babila

FURLA

www.furla.com
Chic leather bags and belts in high-fashion, minimalist designs, but with an original twist. Also scarves and shoes. Affordable prices.
✚ H5 ✉ Piazza Duomo 31, 20122 ☎ 02 8909 6794 Ⓜ San Babila

GIOVANNI GALLI

www.giovannigalli.com
The shop for those who love all things sweet. The *marrons glacés* are legendary, and the traditional sweets and biscuits are good, too. There's another branch in Via Victor Hugo.
✚ H7 ✉ Corso di Porta Romana 2, 20122
☎ 02 8645 3112 Ⓜ Missori

LIBRERIA HOEPLI

www.hoepli.it
Established in 1870, this bookshop, extending over six floors, has the most extensive stock in Milan of books in any language, on any subject.
✚ H5 ✉ Via Hoepli 5, 20121 ☎ 02 864 871 Ⓜ Duomo

LIU.JO

www.liujo.it
Youthful and alluring styles with a hint of femininity. The range of accessories adds the perfect finishing touch.
✚ J5 ✉ Corso Vittorio Emanuele 30, 20122
☎ 02 7631 7658 Ⓜ San Babila

PECK STOPANNI

www.peck.it
Milan's most prestigious delicatessen, with

DEPARTMENT STORES

Department stores are still rather alien to most Italians and Milan has only a handful. The best department store is La Rinascente (www.larinascente.it ✚ H5 ✉ Piazza Duomo ☎ 02 866 371), a monumental shop opposite the Duomo. It stretches over six floors and sells almost everything you could possibly want. Coin (www.coin.it ✚ K6 ✉ Piazza Cinque Giornate 1/a ☎ 02 5519 2083) is also good, and sells a full range of quality products.

numerous stalls specializing in bread, cheese, seafood, salami, marinated vegetables and other delights.
✝ G6 ✉ Via Spadari 9, 20123 ☎ 02 802 3161
🚇 Duomo

PRADA
www.prada.com
This flagship branch of Prada has graced a thousand fashion photographs; the window displays are fabulous.

✝ H5 ✉ Galleria Vittorio Emanuele II 63, 20121 ☎ 02 876 979
🚇 Duomo

RICORDI MEGASTORE
One of Italy's best music stores, selling books on composers and their works, recorded music and sheet music, plus instruments. Concert tickets are also available.
✝ H5 ✉ Galleria Vittorio Emanuele II, 20121

☎ 02 8646 0272
🚇 Duomo

SISLEY
www.sisley.com
This Italian designer's window displays draw the shoppers in droves. Come here to find quality men's shirts, ladies' T-shirts and the latest lingerie.
✝ H6 ✉ Galleria Passerella, Corso Vittorio Emanuele
☎ 02 390 0872
🚇 San Babila

Entertainment and Nightlife

LE BANQUE
www.lebanque.it
A popular nightspot in a former bank. A range of music fills the dance floor, which was once the bank's vault. Happy hour at 6pm weekdays.
✝ G5 ✉ Via E. Porrone 6, 20121 ☎ 02 8699 6565
🚇 Cordusio

CINEMA ODEON 5
A huge mainstream cinema in the middle of Milan showing the latest American blockbusters, many in their original language, so you can still catch the latest releases from home. This 10-screen complex has good access for visitors with disabilities.
✝ H5 ✉ Via Santa Radegonda 8, 20121 ☎ 02 892 111 🚇 Duomo

TEATRO ALLA SCALA
www.teatroallascala.org
Opera, classical and the occasional musical boom out from Milan's, and possibly the world's, most prestigious playhouse. It's not just famous names at La Scala; Maria Callas

THE BIG SCREEN

Going to the cinema is a popular pastime for the Milanese and there are a number of cinemas close to the city center. There are also multiplexes farther out: Arcadia (www.arcadiacinema.com ☎ 02 9541 6445), 28km (18 miles) east of the city at Melzo, is part of a huge site with shops and restaurants, and houses Energia, the biggest screen in Italy.

was unknown when she made her debut here. The venue has a bar, museum, visitor area and an excellent bookshop with many titles in English.
✝ H5 ✉ Piazza della Scala, 20121 ☎ 02 7200 3744
🚇 Duomo/Cordusio

TEATRO NUOVO
www.teatronouvo.it
All types of plays are staged here, including some excellent comedy, musicals and dance productions. There is capacity for more than 1,000 people, who come to see performances by some of the famous actors who appear here on a regular basis.
✝ J5 ✉ Piazza San Babila, 20121 ☎ 02 7600 0086
🚇 San Babila

PRICES

Prices are approximate, based on a 3-course meal for one person.

€€€   over €50
€€   €20–€50
€   under €20

AGNELLO (€€)

www.ristoranteagnello.it
Nothing at Agnello has changed over the years, including its popularity; the central location and very tasty pizzas are the main reasons but the risottos are particularly good, too.

➕ H5   ✉ Via Agnello 8 ☎ 02 8909 6673 🕐 Wed–Mon lunch, dinner 🚇 Duomo

AL MERCANTE (€€)

www.ristorantealmercante.it
Eat outside in summer at this restaurant in one of the most attractive medieval squares in Milan. Tasty pasta, meat and fish, and a good wine list.

➕ G6   ✉ Piazza Mercanti 17, 20123   ☎ 02 805 2198 🕐 Mon–Sat lunch, dinner 🚇 Duomo, Cordusio

BOEUCC (€€€)

www.boeucc.it
It's worth splashing out for a special occasion here, Milan's oldest restaurant, opened in 1696. Stone fluted pillars, oriental rugs and soft lights provide an elegant setting to enjoy excellent Milanese cooking. Or you can choose to eat in the garden in fine weather.

➕ H5   ✉ Piazza Belgioioso 2, 20121   ☎ 02 7602 0224 🕐 Mon–Fri lunch, dinner; Sun dinner only 🚇 Duomo

CAFFÈ MERCANTI (€)

At this café/bar, seating is either in the upper balcony area, with mirrors and chandeliers, or outside under canopies with heaters. Good snacks such as *panini* and salads.

➕ G6   ✉ Via dei Mercanti 21, 20123   ☎ 02 7208 0394 🕐 Daily 6–1 🚇 Cordusio

CAFFÉ VICTOR HUGO (€–€€)

The lovely window displays of dolls and tea sets will tempt you inside this pretty café for a bite to eat or a coffee. Gallery seating area.

A PLETHORA OF PIZZA

There's pizza and there's pizza. Every city in the world produces this famous Italian dish but it never tastes the same as in the country of its birth and you will find some of the best in Milan. Seek out the pizzerias where the food is cooked in the traditional manner in wood-fired ovens (*forno a legna*). They are usually thin crust and made from age-old recipes, and the best ones are normally prepared by one of the many Neapolitan chefs working in the city. A true Italian pizza does not include exotic toppings such as pineapple or corn.

➕ G6   ✉ Via Spadari ☎ 02 869 3614 🕐 Daily 7.30am–8pm 🚇 Cordusio

CAMPARINO IN GALLERIA (€€)

www.caffemiani.it
Famous Milan bar, owned by the Miani family, with an outside terrace ideally placed for people-watching. Prepare to pay a high price for your Negroni or Campari Americano, as you'd expect in Milan's smartest location.

➕ H6   ✉ Galleria Vittorio Emanuele II/Piazza Duomo 21, 20121   ☎ 02 8646 4435 🕐 Tue–Sun. Closed Aug 🚇 Duomo

CHARLESTON (€)

www.ristorantecharleston.it
In the heart of the shopping area, serving a wide variety of pizza plus some interesting Florentine dishes. Dine under the gazebo in summer.

➕ H5   ✉ Piazza Liberty 8, 20121   ☎ 02 798 631 🕐 Daily 🚇 Duomo, San Babila

CRACCO (€€€)

www.ristorantecracco.it
Modern Italian cuisine cooked with the finest and freshest ingredients have given Carlo Cracco's restaurant an international reputation. Reservations advised.

➕ G6   ✉ Via Victor Hugo 4, 20123   ☎ 02 876 774 🕐 Mon–Fri lunch, dinner; Sat dinner only. Closed 2 weeks Aug 🚇 Duomo

DI GENNARO (€)

www.di-gennaro.it
Not far from the Duomo and good for an after-show meal, this pizzeria has been producing classics from the old-fashioned tiled oven for many years.
✚ H5 ✉ Via Santa Radegonda 14, 20121 ☎ 02 805 3454 🕔 Fri–Wed all day 🚇 Duomo

IL GABBIANO (€)

Near the Duomo, this *gelateria* sells milkshakes and fruit salad as well as a large selection of ice cream and sorbets. You can also sit outside.
✚ H5 ✉ Via Ugo Foscolo 3, 20121 ☎ 02 7202 2411 🕔 Daily 🚇 Duomo

MARCHESI (€)

www.pasticceriamarchesi.it
Enjoy the pastries, tarts, salads and much more at this Milan institution. Take away some sweets, cakes or chocolates—the gift-wrapping is a joy.
✚ F5 ✉ Via Santa Maria alla Porta 11a, 20123 ☎ 02 876 730 🕔 Mon–Sat 7.30am–8pm, Sun 8.30–1 🚇 Cordusio, Cairoli

SANT'AMBROEUS (€€)

www.santambroeus.org
The ultimate pastry shop that oozes class. Wonderful window displays of hand-made treats and chocolates get the taste buds going. Beautiful tearoom and tables outside. Sant'Ambroeus is also an

elegant restaurant serving updated traditional dishes from Piedmont.
✚ J5 ✉ Corso Matteotti 7, 20121 ☎ 02 7600 0540 🕔 Daily, closed 3 weeks Aug 🚇 San Babila

SAVINI (€€€)

www.savinimilano.it
Legendary restaurant that has been serving meals since 1867, especially to the rich and famous. The well-prepared food, based on the finest ingredients, lives up to the best Milanese traditions, and this is the most stylish place in Milan to be seen. You'll probably need to have your concierge make your dinner reservation.
✚ H5 ✉ Galleria Vittorio Emanuele II, 20121 ☎ 02 7200 3433 🕔 Daily lunch, dinner. Closed 3 weeks Aug 🚇 Duomo

MILANESE COOKING

The cuisine of Milan and the Lombardy region has a long tradition and remains popular today. Dishes that appear on most menus include the *risotto allo zafferano* (rice cooked with saffron), minestrone soup, polenta *pasticciata* (polenta pie with cheese sauce and white truffles), *costoletta alla milanese* (breaded veal cutlet), *osso buco alla milanese* (veal stewed with the marrow bone) and *rostin negaa* (veal chops in white wine).

TRATTORIA MILANESE (€)

For a taste of old Milan, come to this tiny trattoria in the heart of the city. In business for a century, the trattoria reflects the past and the excellent food lives up to the Milanese tradition. The menu is filled with old favorites, prepared without any *nuovo* frills: polenta, excellent gnocchi and risottos.
✚ G6 ✉ Via Santa Marta 11, 20123 ☎ 02 8645 1991 🕔 Wed–Mon lunch, dinner. Closed mid-Jul to Aug 🚇 Cordusio, Missori

VICTORIA CAFFÈ (€€)

www.victoriaristorante.it
Discreet café behind the Piazza della Scala; the perfect spot for a pizza or pasta lunch, an early-evening drink or a nightcap. The menu offers creative takes on regional dishes, and a specialty is the impeccably fresh tuna tartare. You may spot artists from La Scala at the next table.
✚ G5 ✉ Via Clerici 1, 20121 ☎ 02 869 0792 🕔 Daily 🚇 Duomo

YAR (€€€)

Milan's only dedicated Russian restaurant. Pricey, but the fixed-price menu is less expensive. Dried smoked fish, *borscht* and deer steak.
✚ H8 ✉ Via Giuseppe Mercalli 22, 20122 ☎ 02 5830 5234 🕔 Mon–Sat dinner only 🚇 Missori

CENTRO STORICO RESTAURANTS

This attractive quarter of Milan is dominated by Parco Sempione and the austere Castello Sforzesco. In complete contrast, the bohemian Brera offers medieval streets, restaurants and bars.

2
3
4
5
6
D
E
Via G Verga
Via G
Via C
Cesariano
Piazza E L Morselli
Canonica
Cagnola
MELZI
D'ERIL
F
VIA
CANOVA
CORSO SEMPIONE
VIA A BERTANI
Via G Randaccio
Via
Via G Gherardini
Piermarini
D
A A
Via G F
Via
Sempione I
P
Sempione I
Cirillo
L
D
Via
Sangiorgio
Piazza Sempione
Guerrazzi
Arco della Pace
Porta Sempione
Viale
Corpus Domini
Via N Machiavelli
VIA MARIO PAGANO
Milton / Canova
Napoleone III
Parco Sempione
Via Vincenzo Monti
5 Alpini
Largo V Alpini
5 Alpini
VIA
Via G Revere
VIALE G MILTON
Via
VIALE EMILIO ALEMAGNA
VIA MOLIERE
Viale P e M Curie
Palazzo dell'Arte (Triennale)
Via
L ARIOSTO
Mascheroni
Petrarca
Vincenzo
Via T Tasso
Tamburini
20 Settembre
Monti
Zola
VIA PIETRO PALEOCAPA
Via S Jacini
PIAZ
Piazza N Tommaseo
Via Pontebba
V Spluga
Settembre
Via
Saffi
Via
MILANO NORD CADORNA
Cadorna Staz Nord
Piazza L Cadorna
Cadorna FN Triennale
VIA B G Bazzoni
Via L Mascheroni
XX
Via
V G Rovani
Via V Gioberti
Virgilio
Metastasio
C
Leopardi
Piazza d Conciliazione
Conciliazione
Sebeto
Piazza Italia
G
Boccaccio
Piazza Virgilio
Virgilio
CARDUCCI
S Nicolao
Via Nicolao
VIA E TOTI
Via
Cenacolo Vinciano
Via Flli Ruffini
Caradosso
Vincenzo Monti
Carducci
Largo P d'Ancona
Santa Maria delle Grazie
S Maria delle Grazie
Piazza S Maria delle Grazie
Corso Magenta
P
Nirone
Baracca
Piazzale F Baracca
CORSO
Via M Bandello
Via B Zenale
MAGENTA
Via A De Togni
Via E Panzacchi
VIA
Via Terraggio
Via S Agnese
VIALE DI PORTA VERCELLINA
Via San Vittore
Via M
Palazzo delle Stelline
Via G Marradi
0   250 m
0   250 yds

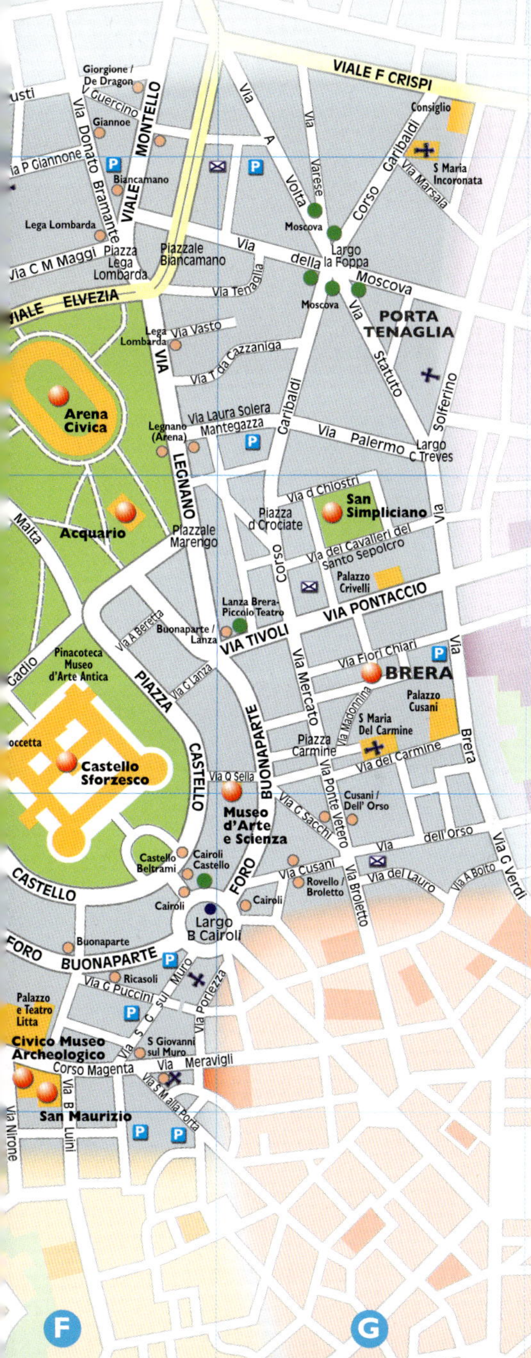
The Northwest

VIALE F CRISPI
Consiglio
Giorgione / De Dragon
V Guercino
Giannoe
MONTELLO
Via P Giannone
VIALE
Donato Bramante
Biancamano
Lega Lombarda
Via C M Maggi
PIAZZA Lega Lombarda
Piazzale Biancamano
Via Tenaglia
VIALE ELVEZIA
Lega Lombarda
Via Vasto
Via T da Cazzaniga
Arena Civica
VIA
LEGNANO
Via Laura Solera Mantegazza
Legnano (Arena)
Acquario
Malta
Piazzale Marengo
A
Via
Volta
Varese
Moscova
Largo della la Foppa
Moscova
Moscova
Garibaldi
Corso
Via Marsala
S Maria Incoronata
PORTA TENAGLIA
Statuto
Solferino
Garibaldi
Via Palermo
Largo C Treves
Via d Chiostri
Piazza d Crociate
San Simpliciano
Via dei Cavalieri del Santo Sepolcro
Corso
Palazzo Crivelli
VIA PONTACCIO
Lanza Brera- Piccolo Teatro
Buonaparte / Lanza
VIA TIVOLI
Via G Lanza
Via A Beretta
Pinacoteca Museo d'Arte Antica
Cadio
PIAZZA
CASTELLO
occetta
Castello Sforzesco
CASTELLO
Via O Sella
Museo d'Arte e Scienza
BUONAPARTE
Via Mercato
Via Flori Chiari
BRERA
Palazzo Cusani
Via Madonnina
S Maria Del Carmine
Piazza Carmine
Via del Carmine
Brera
Via Ponte Vetero
Via G Sacchi
Cusani / Dell' Orso
dell'Orso
Via
Castello Beltrami
Cairoli Castello
FORO
Via Cusani
Cairoli
Via del Lauro
Via A Boito
Via G Verdi
Rovello / Broletto
Via Broletto
Cairoli
Buonaparte
Largo B Cairoli
FORO BUONAPARTE
Via G Puccini
Ricasoli
Via G sul Muro
Via Porlezza
Palazzo e Teatro Litta
Civico Museo Archeologico
S Giovanni sul Muro
Via S M alla Porta
Via Meravigli
Corso Magenta
Via B
San Maurizio
Via Nirone
Luini

F
G
H

Arco della Pace

Triumphal detail from the impressive Arco della Pace at the north end of Parco Sempione

THE BASICS

+ E3
* Piazza Sempione, 20154 and 20145
* 57, 61; tram 1, 30
* Good

HIGHLIGHTS

● The huge bronze Chariot of Peace (25m/82ft high)
● A distant view from the Parco Sempione
● The initial impact as you approach from Corso Sempione

Milan's triumphal arch was intended as a monument to Napoleon's victories. With his fall from power in 1814, the project came to a standstill and he was never to see its completion.

Napoleon's dream The Arch of Victories, as it was at first known, was finally finished in 1838 under the Austrian Emperor, Ferdinand I. In commemoration of the European Peace Treaty of 1815 he changed the name to the Arch of Peace (Arco della Pace) and made appropriate changes to the bas-reliefs. The formal monument marks the northwest end of the Parco Sempione, and the start of the Corso Sempione, Napoleon's highway to the Simplon Pass.

Monumental construction The arch was designed by Luigi Cagnola and inspired by the arch of Septimius Severus in the Forum in Rome. Work began in 1807, halted in 1814, and resumed in 1826 under Ferdinand I of Austria. The circular piazza around it was redesigned in the 1980s and closed to traffic. The arch is best seen from a distance, preferably from the park side, where you can see the Chariot of Peace on the top of the monument. A face-lift has returned the arch to its former glory and the marble gleams once again.

Beyond the arch The two buildings either side of the arch on the park side were toll houses. Open-air concerts are held in the circular piazza on summer evenings, but otherwise the area is best avoided after dark.

Civico Museo Archeologico

Milan was once a powerful Roman city, and this museum, in the ruins of the Benedictine Maggiore monastery, exhibits some fine examples of Roman sculpture and everyday items.

Moving collections The exhibits were formerly housed in the Castello Sforzesco, in the city's archaeological and numismatic collections. Following World War II, several sections were transferred here, next to the church of San Maurizio, with some remaining in the Castello. The monastery, once the largest women's convent in Milan, was built in the ninth century, rebuilt in the early 16th, and was badly bombed in 1943.

Roman and other finds Fragments of Roman funerary stones, sarcophagi and capitals are arranged around the cloister at the front of the museum, with pride of place going to the Masso di Bormo, a large stone whose carvings date back to the third millennium BC. Inside, a model of Roman Milan (Mediolanum) introduces the Roman collection. The basement is devoted to Greek and Etruscan exhibits and a tiny section to works of art from Gandha-ra (what is now northern Pakistan and Afghanistan). Take a look at the Coppa Trivulzio in the Roman section, which is behind the black screen and quite easy to miss. It is an exquisite late fourth-century goblet in emerald-green glass, carved from a single piece of glass. The Roman Parabiago Plate is a large silver-gilt, embossed patera (weighing 3.5kg/8lb) discovered in 1907, from Parabiago, northwest of Milan.

THE BASICS

✚ F5

✉ Corso Magenta 15, 20123

☎ 02 8844 5208

🕓 Tue–Sun 9–5.30. Closed 1 Jan, 1 May, 25 Dec

🚇 Cadorna, Cairoli

🚌 50, 58, 94; tram 16, 27

♿ Poor; phone ahead

✋ Inexpensive, free daily after 4.30 and Tue after 2

ℹ Small booklets in English, inexpensive

HIGHLIGHTS

- Coppa Trivulzio
- Parabiago Plate
- The torso of Hercules: discovered among ruins of Roman baths on what is now Corso Europa
- *Portrait of Maximin* (mid-3rd-century AD): one of a series of portraits dating from the Roman era

Castello Sforzesco

HIGHLIGHTS

● Mausoleum of Bernabò Visconti (1363), Bonino da Campione
● Salle delle Asse (Room 8), with fresco decoration attributed to Leonardo
● Sala degli Scarlioni (Room 15): Michaelangelo's *Rondanini Pietà* (1554–64) and Gaston de Foix's funerary monument, *Agostini Busti*

TIP

● Lots to see—visit the museums on a wet day, the grounds on a sunny one.

A landmark of Milan, the castle is a vast brick quadrilateral, dominated on the town side by the Filarete Tower. It stands as a symbol of the golden Renaissance age, and today is home to the excellent civic museums.

Through the centuries Built as a fortress by the Visconti family between 1358 and 1368, the castle was all but demolished after their downfall. It was transformed into a Renaissance fort under Francesco Sforza, and his son, who became Duke of Milan, turned it into a sumptuous residence. By the early 19th century, Napoleon had turned what was left of the building into soldiers' quarters. In 1884, the city planned a virtual demolition of the castle, but the architect Luca Beltrami transformed it into a museum.

Exploring the museums Start your visit at the entrance under the Filarete Tower. Beyond the massive Piazza d'Armi is the Renaissance Corte Ducale, residence of the Sforzas, around which the Civiche Raccolte d'Arte Antica is displayed. This rich collection of sculpture spans 12 centuries, from a fourth-century sarcophagus to Michelangelo's *Rondanini*—the highlight of the whole collection. On the upper floor is the furniture collection and the art gallery, whose Italian Renaissance masterpieces include works by Mantegna, Giovanni Bellini, Antonella da Messina and Filippo Lippi, as well as a rich collection of works by Lombard artists. The first and second floors are devoted to the applied arts, which include an outstanding collection of musical instruments and the rare Trivulzio Tapestries, designed by Bramantino. The basement houses the archaeology museum.

THE BASICS

www.milanocastello.it

✚ F4

✉ Piazza Castello, 20121

☎ 02 8846 3700

🕐 Castello: daily 7–6/7. Museums: Tue–Sun 9–5.30. Both closed 1 Jan, Easter, 1 May, 25 Dec

🚇 Cadorna, Cairoli, Lanza

🚌 18, 50, 58, 94; tram 1, 4, 12, 14, 19

♿ Good; some steps

✋ Expensive; free Tue–Thu, Sat–Sun 4.30–5.30, Fri after 2

Corso Magenta

TOP
25

From left: a tram on Corso Magenta; Caffè Litta; imposing facade of Palazzo Litta

THE BASICS

✚ E5

✉ Extending east from Porta Magenta to the junction with Via Meravigli

🍴 Numerous cafés and restaurants

Ⓜ Conciliazione, Cadorna

🚌 18, 67; tram 16, 19

HIGHLIGHTS

● Santa Maria delle Grazie and Leonardo da Vinci's *The Last Supper* (*c.*1495–97) (▷ 72–73)
● Civico Museo Archeologico (▷ 65)
● San Maurizio (▷ 71)
● Bar Magenta—historic café (▷ 77)

Any visit to Milan should include this *corso*, one of Milan's most elegant streets flanked by historic *palazzi* and home to Leonardo da Vinci's *The Last Supper* at the Church of Santa Maria delle Grazie.

Along the old road The oldest trace of civilization here is the Roman tower in the grounds of the Archaeological Museum (▷ 65), the only surviving above-ground section of the city's Roman walls. On the same site are the ruins of the ancient Benedictine Maggiore Monastery, founded in the ninth century and renovated in the early 1500s. The rest of the Corso is more recent, typified by baroque, neoclassical and 19th-century mansions.

Plenty to see This is one of Milan's most affluent districts, a desirable residential and shopping area, with chic boutiques, antiques shops and several historic buildings. The great magnet is the Church of Santa Maria delle Grazie, whose splendid terracotta bulk dominates this section of the Corso. The piazza is normally milling with visitors, awaiting their alloted 15-minute slot for da Vinci's *The Last Supper* in the refectory adjoining the church. Going east, the Palazzo delle Stelline at No. 59, a school for orphans in the 17th century, has been transformed out of recognition into a conference facility and hotel. Beyond the crossroads, you can't miss the large baroque facade of Palazzo Litta (No. 24), now home to the Teatro Litta (▷ 77), and across the road, beyond the Archaeological Museum, the Church of San Maurizio (No. 15) is full of fabulous 16th-century frescoes.

24
FERROVIE DELLO STATO
S, A.

Parco Sempione

Cool and inviting, particularly in summer, the park is popular with locals and visitors

THE BASICS

✚ E4

✉ Piazza Castello–Piazza Sempione (8 entrances around perimeter)

☎ Torre Branca: 02 331 4120

🕒 Park: daily 6.30am–8/9/10/11.30pm depending on season.
Torre Branca: Tue, Thu 9.30pm–1am, Wed 10.30–12.30, 4–6.30, 9.30–1, Fri 2.30–6, 9.30–1, Sat, Sun 10.30–2, 2.30–7.30, 9.30–1; winter hours are shorter; check before visiting. Closed in bad weather

🍴 Cafés in park

🚇 Cadorna, Cairioli, Lanza, Moscova

🚌 43, 57, 61, 94; tram 1, 4, 27

✋ Park free; Torre Branca moderate, over 60s and children under 3 free

HIGHLIGHTS

● Arena Civica
● Torre Branca
● *Bagni Misteriosi*, sculpture by Giorgio de Chirico, found behind the Palazzo dell'Arte
● View of Arco della Pace from the lake

A welcome break from the city noise, with a fine view of the Castello Sforzesco, the Parco Sempione was once part of the vast hunting ground of the Sforza family, who occupied the castle. It became a public park in the late 19th century.

Early uses In the early 1800s the French used the land as an exercise ground for their armed forces. Napoleon had plans to build a great piazza around the castle and turn the whole area into the new heart of the city, but apart from the Arco della Pace (▷ 64) and the Arena Civico (▷ 74) the plans never materialized. The public park, 47ha (116 acres) in size, was begun in 1893 when Emilio Alemagna landscaped the area on the lines of an English park—as was the fashion.

The country in town The gardens stretch from the castle to the Arco della Pace—a landscape of lawns, large trees, winding paths and a lake with a small bridge. On the west side, you can't miss the Torre Branca, a steel tower with a lift that will take you to the top for the best views over the city. Designer Roberto Cavalli has opened a restaurant at the base of the tower (▷ 78). The nearby Palazzo dell'Arte is the permanent site of the Triennale Decorative Arts Exhibition and also houses the Design Museum. The park is dotted with modern sculpture and monuments, has lots to amuse children, including sailing boats on the lake, and there's entertainment in the summer months. Although the park is open late into the evening, it is best avoided after dark.

San Maurizio

Divine art—St. Luke the Evangelist attributed to Vincenzo Foppa

THE BASICS

✠ F5

✉ Corso Magenta 15, 20123

🕐 Tue–Sat 9.30–5.30 (can sometimes close for no reason); closed 1 Jan, 1 May, 25 Dec

🚇 Cadorna

🚌 50, 59; tram 19, 20, 24

♿ Poor

✋ Free

ℹ Guidebooks in Italian only

The unremarkable grey baroque facade of this church on the busy Corso Magenta gives no hint of the glorious interior. Step inside and you are greeted by a riot of beautiful baroque frescoes, decorating every surface.

Important convent The church was built in 1503 for the adjoining Monastero Maggiore, formerly one of the most prestigious monasteries in Milan, and home to Benedictine nuns. The monastery was largely destroyed in the 19th century but is today the site of the Civico Museo Archeologico (▷ 65). A schedule of restoration of the church frescoes has been ongoing since 1986.

Church meets state The church was constructed in two main parts: one hall for the congregation and a larger cloistered hall for the nuns. The two were separated by a partition wall and altar, which face you as you go into the church. The nuns were able to participate in Eucharists celebrated in the public hall through the little doors, which you can see in the arch in the central fresco to the left of the altar; they could also receive Communion through the tiny opening (the *comunichino*) on the right of the altar below the figure of Christ.

Wonderful frescoes On both sides of the partition wall is the *Passion of Christ*. Many of the frescoes were executed by Bernardino Luini (*c.*1480–1532), one of the most prominent Lombard followers of Leonardo da Vinci; the chapels on the left were decorated by his pupils.

HIGHLIGHTS

● Frescoes by Bernardino Luini, including *Life of St. Catherine*

● *The Adoration of the Magi*, Antonio Campi

● Frescoes by unattributed artists

● Classical concerts in the nuns' hall in winter

● Excellent lighting to view the frescoes in detail

Santa Maria delle Grazie

While *The Last Supper* is a real highlight, the church itself should not be missed. Although it was built over a mere 26 years, it gives the impression of being two completely different churches.

Renaissance gem Guiniforte Solari designed the church for the Dominican Order in 1463–90. The contrast of styles between the Dominican late-Gothic nave, with its wealth of decoration, and the pure, harmonious domed apse built by Bramante marks the rapid change that came with the Renaissance. In 1943, a bomb destroyed the cloister, but, miraculously, two of its greatest treasures, *The Last Supper* and the dome, survived.

Glorious architecture The magnificent brick and terra-cotta exterior, crowned by Bramante's grand

Clockwise from top far left: detail from Leonardo da Vinci's The Last Supper; *exterior view of Santa Maria delle Grazie; the fine marble and terra-cotta decoration on the church's dome; detail of the arches at the top of the dome; overall view of the church; ornamentation on the facade*

dome, is best seen from Corso Magenta. From the Renaissance portal, you enter Solari's nave, with its richly decorated arches and vaults. Beyond it, Bramante's apse feels simple in comparison. The beautiful Bramante Cloister, surrounding a garden, is familiarly known as Chiostrino delle Rane after the bronze frogs *(rane)* at the fountain. If a service is in progress, you can reach the cloister via the street entrance on Via Caradosso.

Da Vinci's masterpiece Ludovico Il Moro commissioned this fresco in the refectory adjoining the church in 1494, and it is one of the most famous in the world. Unfortunately the experimental techniques used by da Vinci led to signs of deterioration within 20 years of completing the work. Much restoration has been done to return the painting to its former glory. Booking in advance is compulsory.

THE BASICS

www.cenacolovinciano.org

✝ E5

✉ Piazza Santa Maria delle Grazie, 20123

☎ 02 467 6111

🕐 Basilica Mon–Sat 7–12, 3–7.15, Sun and holidays 7.30–12.30, 3.30–8.45. *The Last Supper* Tue–Sun 8.15–6.45

Ⓜ Conciliazione, Cardorna

🚌 18; tram 16

♿ Good; 3 steps

✋ Church free. *The Last Supper* expensive

❓ Book as early as possible to view *The Last Supper*. Tickets must be picked up 20 min in advance of admission time ☎ Reservations 02 9280 0360

More to See

ACQUARIO

www.acquariocivicomilano.eu
Set in a fine art nouveau building, this excellent aquarium was completed in March 2006. It houses some 150 different species from both marine and freshwater environments. Check out the transparent bridge tank so visitors can look at the fish from all angles.
✚ F4 ✉ Via Gadio 2, 20121 ☎ 02 8844 5392 ◉ Tue–Sun 9–1, 2–5.30 ⓜ Lanza 🚌 57; tram 3, 4, 7, 12 ♿ Good ✋ Free

ARENA CIVICA

This huge amphitheater was built in 1806 by Luigi Canonica to seat 30,000 spectators. It has since hosted soccer games and pop concerts; today it is mainly used for athletic events.
✚ F3 ✉ Viale Giorgio Byron 2, Parco Sempione, 20154 ◉ Open for events only FLanza 🚌 57, 70; tram 3, 4, 12, 14

BRERA DISTRICT

The Brera is one of the oldest and most attractive districts in Milan. For many years this quarter was inhabited by artists and there is still a hint of Bohemia. Via Brera is its liveliest street, popular with the young for its open-air cafés, inviting *trattorie*, galleries, street vendors and late-night bars.
✚ G4 ✉ 20121 🚌 61; tram 1, 27

MUSEO D'ARTE E SCIENZA

www.museoartescienza.com
Near the castle, this fascinating private museum shows you how to tell the difference between genuine and fake antiques—some 2,000 of them.
✚ G4 ✉ Via Q. Sella 4, 20121 ☎ 02 7202 2488 ◉ Mon–Fri 10–6 ⓜ Cairoli, Lanza 🚌 57, 61; tram 3, 4, 12, 14 ♿ None ✋ Free/donation; guided tours expensive

SAN SIMPLICIANO

www.sansimpliciano.it
This handsome basilica is the finest of the churches in the Brera quarter. It was founded in the fourth century, possibly by Sant'Ambrogio, and reconstructed in the 12th century.
✚ G4 ✉ Piazza San Simpliciano 7, 20121 ☎ 02 862 274 ◉ Mon–Fri 9–12, 2.15–7, Sat–Sun 9.30–7 ⓜ Lanza 🚌 57, 61; tram 12, 14 ♿ Good ✋ Free

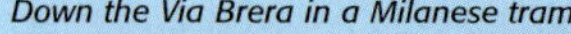
Down the Via Brera in a Milanese tram

Some Milanese Treasures

This gentle walk takes you from the castle via one of the finest churches in the city to the park and into the bohemian Brera district.

DISTANCE: 3.5km (2.2 miles) **ALLOW:** Half a day with stops

START ....

END

CASTELLO SFORZESCO
✚ F4 Ⓜ Cairoli

BRERA DISTRICT
✚ G4 Ⓜ Lanza

❶ Start at the clock tower of the Castello Sforzesco (▷ 66–67). With your back to the castle, follow the path around to the right and cross over the main road into Via Minghetti.

❽ Take the second left into Via Erbe. Cross over Mercato Vetero and you are in the heart of the Brera district, a perfect spot for lunch.

❷ At the end, cross Piazzale Codorna past the station into Via Carducci. Continue until you meet Corso Magenta (▷ 68). Go right and follow the road to Santa Maria delle Grazie (▷ 72–73).

❼ Turning right inside the park takes you back to the castle; left takes you to the triumphal Arco della Pace (▷ 64). At the east side of the park is the Arena Civico (▷ 74) and the Acquario (▷ 74). Exit near here onto Via Gadio and cross into Via Bonaparte.

❸ The adjoining refectory contains da Vinci's famous *The Last Supper* (▷ 72–73). Across the piazza, just past the church, turn into Via Ruffini.

❻ Enter through the gate between the Palazzo dell'Arte (▷ 70) and the Eiffel Tower–like building the Torre Branca (▷ 70), and this will bring you into the main body of the park.

❹ Turn right into Piazza Italia. Cross over and go right into Via Saffi. At the end turn left and continue round into Viale P. e M. Curie and over the railway line.

❺ At the end, cross the road to enter Parco Sempione (▷ 70) opposite.

Shopping

10 CORSO COMO

www.10corsocomo.com
For sheer style don't miss this fabulous store on the fashionable Corso Como. A stunning array of men's and women's fashions, accessories, homewares, books and CDs and something for the little ones, too. Restaurant, B&B and library on the premises as well.
G2 ✉ Corso Como 10, 20154 ☎ 02 2900 2674 Ⓜ Garibaldi

ATRIBU

See and buy the works of young designers before they become household names.
G4 ✉ Corso Giuseppe Garibaldi 49, 20124 ☎ 02 867 127 Ⓜ Lanza

BUSCEMI DISCHI

www.buscemi.com
One of the city's oldest and most famous record stores, split between two shops. Don't hesitate to ask for assistance if you can't find what you want on the crammed shelves.
F5 ✉ Corso Magenta 31, 20123 ☎ 02 804 103 Ⓜ Cadorna

CARTOLERIA RUFFINI

See the craftsmen at work out the back producing handmade notebooks, albums, boxes and letter racks, which are then sold at the front of this traditional old shop.
E5 ✉ Via Ruffini 1, 20123 ☎ 02 463 074 Ⓜ Conciliazione

DIEGO DELLA PALMA

www.diegodallapalma.com
Lipsticks, powders and paints from this household name among Italy's make-up elite. Knowledgeable staff can advise you on the products to use to suit your skin tone.
G4 ✉ Via Madonnina 15, 20121 ☎ 02 876 818 Ⓜ Lanza

E.E. ERCOLESSI

www.ercolessi.gpa.it
For the complete pen experience, visit this family business that has been in Milan since 1921. Large wooden cabinets hold the extensive range of pens ranging from familiar brands to limited editions, and the company's marble green signature pen.
E5 ✉ Corso Magenta 25, 20123 ☎ 02 8645 2444 Ⓜ Cadorna

LA FUNGHERIA

www.lafungheria.com
To the west of Corso Magenta you will find quality mushrooms and truffles in this shop, known in Milan for its organic methods. It's worth the little extra journey to get that slightly more unusual gift to take home.
B5 ✉ Via Marghera 14, 20149 ☎ 02 439 0089 Ⓜ Wagner, De Angeli

LUISA BECCARIA

www.luisabeccaria.com
Delicate satin and chiffon feature in this Milanese designer's dreamy, feminine styles.
G4 ✉ Via Formentini 1, 20121 ☎ 02 8646 0018 Ⓜ Lanza

MERCATO D'ANTIQUARIATO DI BRERA

Enthusiasts should not miss this monthly antiques market of about 60 stalls laden with collectibles at bargain prices.
G4 ✉ Via Fiori Chiari, 20121 🕐 3rd Sun of month 8.30–6 Ⓜ Lanza

OLD ENGLISH FURNITURE

www.gracis.com
If you like 18th- and 19th-century English furniture, head for this shop, which has many graceful examples on display.
G4 ✉ Via San Simpliciano 6, 20121 ☎ 02 877 807 Ⓜ Lanza

Entertainment and Nightlife

BAR MAGENTA

Friendly staff, wooden tables and a top shelf stacked full of the world's finest spirits. Every type of music from jazz to rock and punk is played on the bar's stereo system. Popular with students and fans of sport—particularly Italian football—so it can get noisy.

✚ F5   ✉ Via Carducci 13, 20123   ☎ 02 8053 3808   Ⓜ Cordusio

CRT TEATRO DELL'ARTE

www.crtmilano.it
Most performances are in Italian but the passionate music and contemporary dance displays will need no translation. Several yearly dance festivals with top directors, dancers and actors.

✚ E4   ✉ Viale Alemagna 6, 20121   ☎ 02 8901 1644   Ⓜ Cadorna

GLORIA MULTISALA

www.multisalagloria.it
This renovated cinema comprises two theaters, the Garbo and the Marilyn. Both have big screens and a good sound system. Bar.

✚ D5   ✉ Corso Vercelli 18, 20144   ☎ 02 4800 8908   Ⓜ Pagano, Conciliazione

HOLLYWOOD

www.discotecahollywood.it
Getting in is neither cheap nor easy—you'll need lots of cash and your latest Galleria Emanuele outfit. But once inside you could be rubbing shoulders with Milan's beautiful people.

✚ G2   ✉ Corso Como 15, 20154   ☎ 02 659 8996   Ⓜ Garibaldi

JAMAICA

www.jamaicabar.it
Since 1920, Brera's painters and artists have flocked to this legendary haunt, and it's still popular today. The cocktails and huge salads are good.

✚ G4   ✉ Via Brera 32, 20121   ☎ 02 876 723   Ⓜ Montenapoleone

OLD FASHION CAFÉ

www.oldfashion.it
Exclusive nightspot in a former ballroom that attracts a chic crowd to its theme nights.

✚ E4   ✉ Viale E. Alemagna 6, 20121   ☎ 02 805 6231   Ⓜ Cadorna

TEATRO DAL VERME

www.dalverme.org
The small theater has a full schedule of classical and semi-classical concerts and chamber music performed by both touring groups and local musicians.

✚ F5   ✉ Via San Giovanni sul Muro 2, 20121   ☎ 02 87905   Ⓜ Cairoli

TEATRO LITTA

www.teatrolitta.it
Children's plays make up the lion's share of performances in this theater, in the striking Palazzo Litta. The magic and dance displays will delight English-speaking kids, although the Italian drama shows may be beyond them. A peek inside the classic baroque theater is worth it for those interested in architecture.

✚ F5   ✉ Corso Magenta 24, 20123   ☎ 02 8645 4545   Ⓜ Cadorna

TOCQUEVILLE 13

www.tocqueville13milano.com
It may be named after the famous political thinker, but it's celebrity-spotting the punters come for on the club's ultracool party nights. Feast on tapas all night.

✚ G2   ✉ Via de Tocqueville 13, 20154   ☎ 02 2900 2973   Ⓜ Garibaldi

DANCING TRENDS

Milan is the place to be if you are on the lookout for new music and dance trends. The city boasts hordes of discos and clubs that offer all types of music but the trend tends to lean toward a select few. Apart from the rare exceptions, clubs and discos change their name and style on a regular basis. A club that is in vogue one week can be passé the next. Entrance fees vary a lot—a system known as "drinkcard", where you pay for your drinks at the door, is often used. Some places are free to get in but you will pay, probably over the top, for drinks.

Restaurants

PRICES

Prices are approximate, based on a 3-course meal for one person.

€€€ over €50
€€ €20–€50
€ under €20

ALICE RESTAURANT (€€–€€€)

www.aliceristorante.it
On the second floor of Eataly Milano Smeraldo, Alice is part of a complex that combines fine dining, a specialty grocery store and venue for food and cultural events.
G2 Piazza XXV Aprile 10, 20121 02 4949 7301 Mon–Sat 12–2.30, 7–11 Muscova, Garibaldi

BIFFI (€€)

www.biffipasticceria.it
Biffi has been around since the end of the 19th century and is the place to try their own *panettone*. Come here for breakfast before shopping.
D5 Corso Magenta 87, 20123 02 4800 6702 Tue–Sun Conciliazione

BINDI (€)

For mouthwatering cream cakes and pastries drop in at this bright and cheery local café, close to the castle and park.
F5 Piazale Cadorna 9, 20123 02 8645 1178 Mon–Sat Cadorna

C'ERA UNA VOLTA (€€)

The atmosphere at this trattoria changes with the time of day: lunch is relaxed, loud and crowded with office workers; for dinner it's tablecloths, candles and couples sharing a romantic meal. Good pasta and fish dishes.
G3 Via Palermo 20, 20121 02 654 060 Mon–Sat lunch, dinner Moscova

JUST CAVALLI CAFÉ (€€€)

www.milano.cavalliclub.com
Designer Roberto Cavalli's hot spot at the base of the Torre Branca. The semicircular steel and glass structure encloses a sophisticated restaurant with animal print accessories. Sip cocktails with celebrities and eat dishes from worldwide cuisines. Garden with a gazebo.
E4 Viale Luigi Cameons, Torre Branca, 20121 02 311 817 Mon–Sat dinner Cadorna

REGIONAL FISH DISHES

Although Milan does not have a typical Lombardy cuisine, it has embraced the cooking of the surrounding area. The fish market in Milan is one of the finest in Italy, and you will find the freshest fish and seafood on many restaurant menus. A visit to the lakes gives you the chance to sample some good local fish, such as carp or tench, while the restaurants close to the River Po serve eel and catfish.

L'OSTERIA DI BRERA (€€–€€€)

www.osteriadibrera.it
In one of the most picturesque streets in the Brera district, impeccably fresh seafood is stylishly presented amid white linens and crystal.
G4 Via Fiori Chiari 8, 20121 02 8909 6628 Daily noon–midnight Cadorna

ROCKING HORSE (€€)

At the north end of Corso Como, this is a nice place to eat salads, pizzas and pastas alfresco.
G2 Corso Como 12 , 20154 02 657 0433 Daily lunch, dinner Garibaldi

SHOCKOLAT (€)

www.shockolat.it
Gelato in many shades of chocolate and other flavors as well. On a weekend you'll have to stand in line as this place is no secret.
E5 Via Giovanni Boccaccio, 20123 02 4810 0597 Daily to 1am Cadorna

SOPHIA'S (€€€)

www.sophiarestaurant.com
A red marble staircase with a crystal handrail sets the tone at this refined restaurant in a renovated loft. Enjoy a combination of creative and traditional Mediterranean dishes.
D2 Enterprise Hotel, Corso Sempione 91, 20154 02 3181 8855 Daily lunch, dinner 1, 11, 19

Probably not the most visited part of the city, but this area features some of the most striking churches in Milan, medieval remains, quiet piazzas and the bohemian shopping street of Corso di Porto Ticinese.

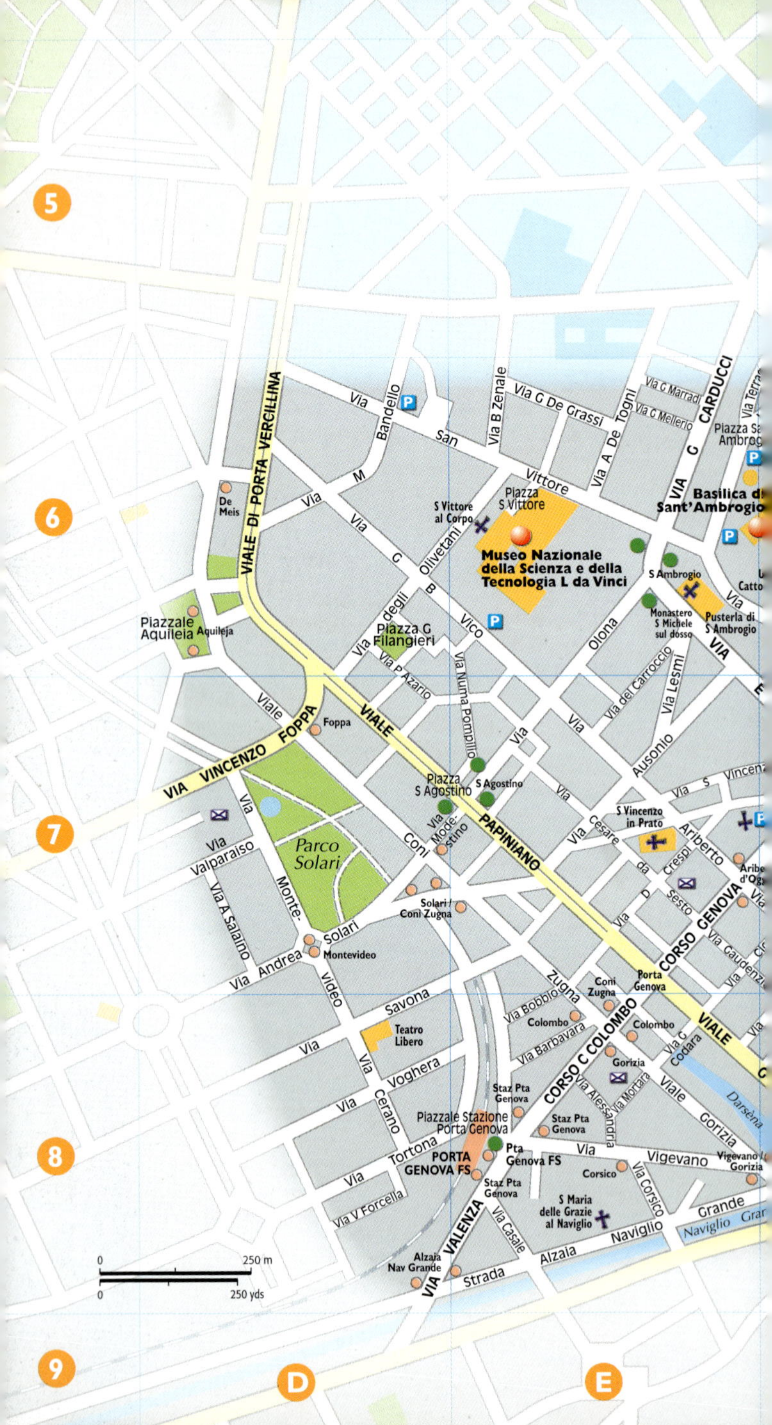

5
6
7
8
9
D
E
Via G Marradi
Via Terra
Via G De Grassi
Via B Zenale
Via A De Togni
Via C Mellerio
CARDUCCI
VIA G
Piazza Sa
Ambrog
Via
Bandello
P
Via
San
Vittore
VIA DI PORTA VERCELLINA
Via
M
Via
G
Via
degli
Olivetani
B
Vico
De Meis
Basilica di
Sant'Ambrogio
S Vittore
al Corpo
Piazza
S Vittore
Museo Nazionale
della Scienza e della
Tecnologia L da Vinci
S Ambrogio
Catto
VIA
Monastero
S Michele
sul dosso
Pusterla di
S Ambrogio
P
Piazzale
Aquileia
Aquileja
Piazza G
Filangieri
Via P Azario
Via Numa Pompilio
Olona
Via dei Carroccio
Via Lesmi
Ausonio
Vincen
Viale
Foppa
Foppa
VIA VINCENZO FOPPA
VIALE
Via
Piazza
S Agostino
S Agostino
Via
Via
Via
Cesare
PAPINIANO
S Vincenzo
in Prato
Ariberto
Via S
P
Aribe
d'Og
Via
Valparaiso
Via
Parco
Solari
Coni
Via
Mode-
stino
da
Crespi
sesto
CORSO GENOVA
Via Caudenzi
Ci
Via A Salaino
Monte-
Solari
Montevideo
Solari
Coni Zugna
Via
Andrea
video
Savona
Zugna
Via Bobbio
Coni
Zugna
Porta
Genova
Via
Colombo
Colombo
VIALE
Via
Voghera
Teatro
Libero
Via Barbavara
CORSO C COLOMBO
Gorizia
Via G
Codara
Viale
Gorizia
Darsena
Via
Cerano
Via Alessandra
Via Mortara
Staz Pta
Genova
Piazzale Stazione
Porta Genova
Pta
Genova FS
Staz Pta
Genova
Via
Vigevano
Vigevano /
Gorizia
Via
Tortona
PORTA
GENOVA FS
Corsico
Via Corsico
Via
Staz Pta
Genova
S Maria
delle Grazie
al Naviglio
Grande
Via V Forcella
VIA VALENZA
Via Casale
Alzaia
Naviglio
Naviglio Gran
Alzaia
Nav Grande
Strada
250 m
250 yds
0
0

Via Agnese
Via Nirone
Via Valeria
Via Corani
Via Borromel
Largo A E A Gemelli
Via S
Via L Necchi
Palazzo Stanga
Via Cappuccio
Palazzo Borromeo
Piazza Borromeo
Via S Orsola
Univ Cattolica
Via S Pio V
Palazzo Visconti
Piazza Mentana
Via Marta
Via Circo
Via S Sisto
Via Medici
Via Nerino
Piazza S Giorgio
Torino
Lanzone
San Bernardino
Largo del Carrobbio
Carrobbio / S Maria Valle
Via S M Valle
Largo Gallarati
Ars
Via Caminadella
Correnti-Carrobbio
Via C Correnti
Ticenese Carrobbio
Via di Porta Ticinese
Stampa
Vito
Piazza della Resistenza Partigiana
Resistenza Partigiana
Via C G Mora
Via Fabbri
Piazza d Vetra
Piazza Salvatore Quasimodo
Via d Chiusa
Via Torti
AMICIS
Corso di Porta Ticinese
Colonne di S Lorenzo
San Lorenzo Maggiore
VIA MOLINO DELLE ARMI
Via Conca del Naviglio
S M Vittoria
Molino delle Armi
Ticinese
Parco delle Basiliche
Via A Banfi
Croce
Via Vettabbia
Anfiteatro Romano
Arena
Via
Vetere
Simonetta
d'Oggiono
Via Scaldasole
Corso di Porta Ticinese
Via Ronzoni
Via P Panzeri
Corso di Porta
Museo Diocesano
Santa
Via Calatafimi
S Eustorgio / 24 Maggio
Basilica di Sant'Eustorgio
D'ANNUNZIO
Piazza S Eustorgio
Via Sambuco
Porta Ticinese
VIALE GIAN GALEAZZO
Piazza XXIV Maggio
F
G

Basilica di Sant'Ambrogio

Named for the patron saint of Milan, Sant'Ambrogio is a supreme example of Romanesque architecture and a prototype for 11th- and 12th-century churches all over Lombardy.

Years in the building The church, west of the Duomo, was originally built between AD379 and 386 by Bishop Ambrogio, who was later made patron saint of Milan. The church was enlarged in the ninth and 11th centuries, although Bramante's Portico della Canonica was left unfinished until the 17th century, and had to be reconstructed after the 1943 bombings.

Superb decoration This is one of the loveliest churches in the city, occupying a large complex with lots to see. The fine redbrick exterior,

with its two bell towers (ninth-century one to the right, 12th-century one to the left) is best seen from Piazza Sant'Ambrogio. Access to the church is via the lovely Ansperto atrium, which was built as a refuge for pilgrims. The church interior, simple and harmonious, has three aisles and distinctive ribbed cross vaulting. The apse is embellished with mosaics (sixth- to eighth-century, much restored) depicting Christ between Milanese saints and martyrs.

Not to be missed Beautifully carved in the fourth century, the Sarcophagus of Stilicho, below the pulpit and left of the nave, is traditionally believed to be the tomb of the Roman military commander Stilicho and his wife and is one of the few surviving features of the original church. The pulpit above it was constructed from 12th-century fragments.

THE BASICS

www.basilicasantam-brogio.it

✚ F6

✉ Piazza Sant'Ambrogio 15, 20123

☎ 02 8645 0895

🕐 Mon–Sat 10–12, 2.30–6, Sun 3–5. No visits during services

🚇 Sant'Ambrogio

🚌 50, 58, 94

♿ Good

✋ Free; Chapel of San Vittore in Ciel d'Oro inexpensive

Museo Nazionale della Scienza e della Tecnologia

TOP 25

The Museo Nazionale della Scienza e della Tecnologia "Leonardo da Vinci" is one of the world's largest science and technology museums, with around 10,000 scientific exhibits and displays.

Early beginnings The oldest of the three museum buildings (the Monumental Building) is the Olivetan Monastery, built in Renaissance style in the 16th century. Although much has been altered, it still has two beautiful cloisters. The site became a military hospital and barracks under Napoleon. It opened as a museum in 1953 with an exhibition on Leonardo da Vinci, to coincide with the fifth centenary of his birth.

Vast collections Within the labyrinthine museum are 16 interactive laboratories where visitors can

learn all about science and technology, including cutting-edge issues such as robotics and bio-technology; children especially enjoy the hands-on approach. There are also two separate buildings, devoted to rail, air and sea transport: steam and electric trains are in the reconstructed art nouveau station (the Train Pavilion), while aircraft and ships can be found in the Aero-Maritime Pavilion.

Planning your visit This museum can appear vast and daunting the first time you come so decide what you most want to see before your visit. The Leonardo Gallery is fascinating, though most of the explanations are in Italian only. If you take children, it's best to head for the interactive labs, huge boats, steam trains and aircraft. You can also visit the submarine *Toti* outside the Monumental Building.

THE BASICS

www.museoscienza.org

✚ E6

✉ Via San Vittore 21, 20123

☎ 02 485 551

🕐 Tue–Fri 10–6, Sat and holidays 10–7. Closed 1 Jan, 24 and 25 Dec

🍴 Refreshment area

🚇 Sant'Ambrogio

🚌 50, 58, 94

♿ Good

✋ Expensive

❓ Submarine *Toti* tours may be unavailable because of heat or cold

San Lorenzo Maggiore

A replica of the Roman statue of Constantine (left) and a good meeting place (below)

THE BASICS

www.sanlorenzomaggiore.com

☩ F7

✉ Corso di Porta Ticinese 35, 20123

☎ 02 8940 4129

🕐 Basilica Mon–Sat 7.30–6.45, Sun 9–7. Museum daily 10–6

Ⓜ Missori

🚌 94; tram 3, 15

♿ Good

✋ Free; Capella di Sant'Aquilino inexpensive

HIGHLIGHTS

● Capella di Sant'Aquilino
● Fourth/fifth-century mosaics
● 12th-century fresco
● The view of the church from Parco delle Basiliche, the garden behind the church

This huge fourth-century basilica may have been the chapel of the imperial Roman palace. The greatest treasure is the Sant'Aquilino Chapel, once entirely covered in frescoes and mosaics.

Founded on a Roman temple The church can be found in the Ticinese quarter, outside the Roman walls, southwest of the city. It is also known as San Lorenzo alle Colonne, named after the colonnade outside the church, dating from the second and third centuries. The 16 columns and the section of architrave were probably part of a temple and were placed here in the fourth century when construction began on the basilica. Built with marble from Roman buildings nearby, the basilica was founded on what was thought to be a Roman amphitheater. It was subsequently rebuilt in the 12th century, with further rebuilding between 1573 and 1619 by Martino Bassi.

Beautiful chapel You can't miss the church—it has the largest dome in Milan. The interior, octagonal in form and crowned by the dome, is striking for its sheer size. Inside, make for the Capella di Sant'Aquilino, which may have been added as a mausoleum; its small chapel houses the saint's remains in a silver urn. The 12th-century fresco of *The Deposition* can be seen at the entrance to the chapel, on the left-hand side. Here you will find the remarkable fourth- or fifth-century mosaics of *Christ and the Apostles*, and *Elijah on the Chariot of Fire*. Steps behind the altar take you down to the foundations of the church.

More to See

BASILICA DI SANT'EUSTORGIO

www.santeustorgio.it

The unassuming neo-Romanesque facade of the Basilica of Sant'Eustorgio belies the wonderful earlier interior architecture and superb frescoes, which make this one of the most interesting churches to visit in the city. The original church was founded by St. Eustorgius in the fourth century but was completely destroyed by Frederick Barbarossa in 1162. Reconstruction began in 1190 and lasted for several centuries. This included the building of the bell tower in 1306, the first in Milan to be fitted with a clock. The final alteration came in 1865 with the building of the facade seen today. The monastery adjoining the church is the property of the Diocesan museum and has 17th- and 18th-century religious relics and art from the Basilica.

✚ F8 ✉ Piazza Sant'Eustorgio 1, 20122 ☎ Church and museum: 02 5810 1583 🕐 Church: Mon–Sat 7.45–5, Sun 9.30–11, 12.30–5; museum: Tue–Sun 10–6 🚌 Tram 3, 9, 29, 30 ♿ Good (ramp to church) ✋ Church free; museum moderate

CORSO DI PORTA TICINESE

This street is bisected by one of the remaining medieval gates surrounding the heart of Milan: Porta Ticinese. This area is popular with younger shoppers as its trendy, retro clothing and accessory boutiques are less expensive than the designer shops farther north. Its bohemian atmosphere makes it a fun place to visit and it also has several good traditional *trattorie*.

✚ F7–F8 ✉ Extends from Lago Carrobbio down to Piazza Eustorgio 🚌 Tram 3

PARCO DELLE BASILICHE

Named after the basilicas of San Lorenzo and Sant'Eustorgio, this is a pleasant park in the southeast of the city. A pathway flanked by roses links the two basilicas—with the busy Via Molino delle Armi in between. Once one of the least desirable spots in the city, where public hangings took place and tanners' workshops created a foul stench, it now fortunately affords a more pleasurable experience.

✚ F7 ✉ Southeast of city, 20123 🕐 Dawn–dusk 🚌 94; tram 3

Porta Ticinese—one of the original gateways to the city, leading to Corso di Porta Ticinese, a hot spot for shopping

Museums to Canals

Begin at one of the city's finest museums, visit churches along the way, retreat to peaceful gardens and finish up by the canals.

DISTANCE: 3.2km (2 miles) **ALLOW:** 2 hours plus stops

START

END

MUSEO NAZIONALE DELLA SCIENZA
✚ E6 Sant'Ambrogio

NAVIGLI
✚ E8 Porta Genova 59; tram 2, 3

❶ If you are keen on science, visit the Museo Nazionale della Scienza (▷ 84–85) in Via San Vittore. Turn right out of the museum and continue along to cross over Via Carducci.

❷ Ahead is the lovely Basilica di Sant'Ambrogio (▷ 82–83). Take the path to the left and follow it right the way round the church. Turn right into Piazza Sant'Ambrogio.

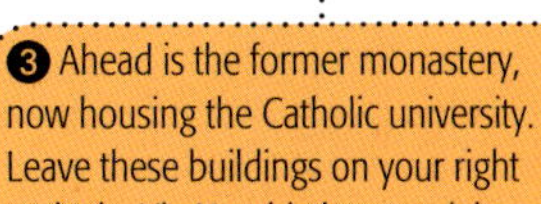

❸ Ahead is the former monastery, now housing the Catholic university. Leave these buildings on your right and take Via Necchi, the next right.

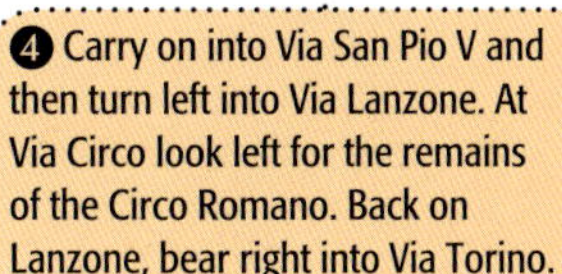

❹ Carry on into Via San Pio V and then turn left into Via Lanzone. At Via Circo look left for the remains of the Circo Romano. Back on Lanzone, bear right into Via Torino.

❽ Turning to the right from the piazza brings you to the Navigli (▷ 96) district, an ideal spot to explore or lunch by the canals.

❼ In the park is the Museo Diocesano, with its fine collection of religious art. At the far end of the park is Sant'Eustorgio (▷ 88). Exit here and turn right alongside the church and then left back onto Corso Ticinese. Carry on down to Piazzale XXIV Maggio.

❻ Continue to San Lorenzo Maggiore (▷ 86) on your left, and on through the Antica Porta Ticinese, the original entry point into the city. Take the first left for a break in the small park (Basiliche ▷ 88).

❺ Cross Lago Carrobbio; take the second right into Corso di Porta Ticinese.

Shopping

ANNA FABIANO

It's nice to find a shop where the clothes are cutting edge but are also wearable in everyday situations. No two pieces are exactly the same and they will definitely get you noticed.

✚ F7 ✉ Corso di Porta Ticinese 40, 20123 ☎ 02 5811 2348 Ⓜ Missori ▯ Tram 2, 3

B-FLY

This customized Levi's shop is a real boon for jeans aficionados. All items have been abused enough with scissors, spray cans and threads to be called one-off. The hand-crafting is reflected in the price.

✚ F7 ✉ Corso di Porta Ticinese 46, 20123 ☎ 02 8942 3178 Ⓜ Missori ▯ Tram 2, 3

BIFFI

www.biffi.com

The place to shop for classic men's and women's designer names; watch for new emerging talent. Clothes for the sporty, younger customer are across the street.

✚ F7 ✉ Corso Genova 6, 20123 ☎ 02 8311 6052 Ⓜ Porta Genova, Sant'Ambrogio

CUSTO

www.custo-barcelona.com

Bold use of tints and printed patterns are evident in the sophisticated designs of this Spanish designer from Barcelona, new to Milan.

✚ F7 ✉ Corsa di Porta Ticinese 58, 20123 ☎ 02 5810 4853 ▯ Tram 2, 3

(ETHIC)

www.ethic.it

Refined casualware with a unique style all of its own, which leans toward an ethnic look using natural materials and dyes. Costume jewelry, too, that follows the same trend.

MARKETS

Milan's street markets are noisy and fun, selling anything from cheeses and salami to clothes and secondhand books, plus there are good specialist markets as well. Markets fill the waterfronts around the canals, notably Mercato del Sabato on Viale Papiniano (✚ E7) on Saturday, which offers great designer-label bargains in clothes, shoes and bags, and there is a flea market (Fiera di Senigallia) at Darsena, on Viale d'Annunzio (✚ F8) also on Saturday. A huge antiques market stretches alongside the canals on the last Sunday of each month. Elsewhere in the city other good general markets are at Via San Marco (✚ G3) on Monday and Thursday mornings, Via Zuretti (✚ Off map at K1) on Wednesday morning and Via Crema (✚ K9) on Friday morning.

✚ F7 ✉ Corso di Porta Ticinese 50, 20123 ☎ 02 5810 5669 ▯ Tram 2, 3

GIORGIO FEDON 1919

www.fedon.it

Smart, elegant and with cleanest of lines, the leather goods at this old-established store are second to none and have prices to match. Optical accessories and quality writing implements on sale too.

✚ F6 ✉ Lago Carrobbio, 20123 ☎ 02 8691 7500 Ⓜ Missori ▯ Tram 2, 3

KALOS

www.kalos-snc.it

Big bold costume jewelry at reasonable prices attractively displayed in a store in the popular shopping street, Porta Ticinese. Rings, bracelets, earrings, necklaces.

✚ F7 ✉ Corso di Porta Ticinese 50, 20123 ☎ 02 8940 4329 Ⓜ Missori ▯ Tram 2, 3

RAPONI

www.tessutiraponi.it

Mouthwatering fabrics in silk, crisp linen, cotton and wool, including fine Italian silks in solid, classic and contemporary patterns, plus needlework accessories, ribbons and trimmings. Even if you don't sew, step in to feast your eyes.

✚ F8 ✉ Vaile d'Annunzio 27, 20123 (corner of Via Panzeri) ☎ 02 8940 4367 Ⓜ XXIV Maggio ▯ Tram 9, 29, 30

LE BICICLETTE
www.lebiciclette.com
Sleek, modern bar and restaurant with changing art exhibitions in an area increasingly popular for nightlife. Happy hour and buffet from 6 until 9.30.
✚ F7 ✉ Via Torti 4, 20123 ☎ 02 5810 4325 Ⓜ Sant'Ambrogio

MAMA CAFÉ RESTAURANT
www.mamacafe.it
A popular restaurant in the day, but the wines and cocktails are the order of the night. On Friday and Saturday nights there is live music of various types.
✚ F7 ✉ Via Caminadella 7, 20123 ☎ 02 8699 5682 Ⓜ Sant'Agostino

OLD FOX PUB
www.oldfoxpub.it
Keeping the original fittings of the former local milk bar, this is the quintessential British pub. Good selection of beers and the owners have a penchant for whiskies. Lots of English pub grub, Italian sports on screen and accompanying music. Occasional theme music nights (check first for details). Buffet and happy hour are very good value from 6 until 9.
✚ E7 ✉ Piazza Sant'Agostino, 20123 ☎ 02 8940 2662 Ⓜ Sant'Agostino

PISCINA SOLARI
www.milanosport.it
Take a dip in this glass-covered five-lane pool, overlooking Parco Solari.
✚ D7 ✉ Via Montevideo 20, 20144 ☎ 02 4695 278 🕐 Times vary, so phone first Ⓜ Sant'Agostino

SCIMMIE
www.scimmie.it
A fantastic, happening venue for jazz, rock, blues, country, folk, flamenco and Brazilian beats, and some international stars appear here. Feast on great-value pizza and snacks as you watch the shows.
✚ F9 ✉ Via Ascanio Sforza 49, 20136 ☎ 02 3981 1039 Ⓜ Porta Genova

MILANESE BARS

From the chic and trendy to the more traditional, Milanese bars are sprinkled throughout the city, and most are open all day until 2 or 3am. They serve a vast selection of beers, wines, aperitifs, cocktails and non-alcoholic drinks, and most have a selection of snacks—some double as cafés. Many of Milan's bars have introduced an early-evening happy hour when drinks are cheaper. If you sit down for waiter service you will pay a premium, whether inside or out. The procedure when standing up is to pay for what you want at the cash desk, then take your receipt to the bar and repeat your order.

SHU
www.shucafe.it
Cool arty restaurant, music/disco bar. Sophisticated interiors and fusion cuisine make this a trendy venue for cocktails and dinner. The bar champions the work of young artists. There is an art events night and various other theme evenings.
✚ G7 ✉ Via Molino delle Armi, 20122 ☎ 02 5831 5720 Ⓜ Missori

TEATRO ARSENALE
www.teatroarsenale.org
The place to come for searing comedy, cutting-edge dramas and groundbreaking acting by up-and-coming thespians. Tickets are available from the venue itself, and can be bought online. Most performances are in Italian only.
✚ F7 ✉ Via Cesare Correnti 11, 20123 ☎ Box office 02 8321 1999, information 02 832 1999 Ⓜ Sant'Ambrogio

LE TROTTOIR
www.letrottoir.it
Not just a bar, Le Trottoir is a platform for creative new talent. There's always something happening here making it a popular student hangout. Events across the spectrum, from live rock bands and jazz artists to poetry readings. Inexpensive cocktails ensure a chilled night out.
✚ Γ8 ✉ Piazza XX1V Maggio 1, 20122 ☎ 02 837 8166 🕐 Daily 11am–late 🚋 Tram 2, 3

Restaurants

PRICES

Prices are approximate, based on a 3-course meal for one person.

€€€ over €50
€€ €20–€50
€ under €20

AMICI DEL LIBERTY (€€)

www.amicidelliberty.com
This Liberty-style dining room creates a romantic setting using rich red shades, ferns and mirrors. Traditional Italian dishes on the menu.

✚ D7 ✉ Via Savona 20, 21044 ☎ 02 839 4302 ◷ Mon–Fri lunch, dinner; Sat dinner. Closed Aug ⊖ Sant'Agostino

CALIFORNIA BAKERY (€)

www.californiabakery.it
In a pleasant spot facing the piazza, this café offers homemade US specialties —bagels, muffins, brownies, cheesecake and more.

✚ F8 ✉ Piazza Sant Eustorgio 4, 20122 ☎ 02 3981 1538 ◷ Daily 9.30–midnight, Sun brunch 12–4 🚌 Tram 2, 3

CANTINA DELLA VETRA (€€)

Venerable, real Italian restaurant, close to the Porta Ticinese. Giant slabs of lasagne, stew, hearty pastas and grilled meats.

✚ G7 ✉ Via Pio IV 3, 20122 ☎ 02 8940 3843 ◷ Mon–Tue, Thu–Fri, Sun dinner, Wed, Sat lunch, Sun brunch at 12 and 2 ⊖ Missori

IL GIARDINETTO (€€)

www.osteriailgiardinetto.it
Warm *osteria* resplendent with plants. Excellent cuisine based on Milanese and Placentina tradition.

✚ E8 ✉ Via Tortona 17, 21044 ☎ 02 839 3807 ◷ Mon–Fri lunch, dinner; Sat dinner ⊖ Sant'Agostino

KAZAN (€–€€)

www.kazansushi.it
Good when you fancy a change from Italian food. Choose from an extensive menu that includes sushi, Japanese noodle and meat dishes and Chinese specialties. Daily lunch and dinner specials are good value.

✚ F7 ✉ Corso di Porta Ticinese 70, 21044 ☎ 02 8366 0979 ◷ Daily 11–3, 6–midnight ⊖ Missori 🚌 Tram 2, 3

TRATTORIA OR OSTERIA?

In general, a trattoria is an unpretentious, family-run concern, often with a regular clientele of local people who drop in when they do not want to cook themselves. The *osteria* used to be the most basic eating place of all, where simple dishes were washed down with jugs of local wine. Nowadays, however, the word has been adopted by some of the most expensive or touristy establishments. Don't judge by the name alone: generally the smarter the premises, the pricier the restaurant.

LANGOSTERIA 10 (€–€€)

Mediterranean tastes show through in both the cuisine and sunny decor, in a relaxed ambience. Seasonal produce.

✚ E7 ✉ Via Savona 10, 21044 ☎ 02 832 2496 ◷ Tue–Sun lunch, dinner; Mon dinner only. Closed Aug ⊖ Sant'Agostino

OSTERIA DEI BINARI (€€)

In summer eat outside in one of the nicest gardens in Milan. Lombardy and Piedmont cooking is the specialty. Friendly service.

✚ E8 ✉ Via Tortona 1/3, 20144 ☎ 02 2839 5095 ◷ Mon–Sat dinner only ⊖ Porta Genova

RISTORANTE SANT' EUSTORGIO (€€)

Nice venue overlooking the square and the church, just off Porta Ticinese. Stop here for a pizza or traditional dish. Good homemade food from fresh local produce.

✚ F8 ✉ Piazza Sant'Eustorgio 6, 20122 ☎ 02 5810 1396 ◷ Daily 12–11.30 ⊖ Missori 🚌 Tram 2, 3

TRATTORIA ALL'ANTICA (€–€€)

Memorable Milanese and Lombard cuisine. Small and very popular, so reserve in advance.

✚ D7 ✉ Via Montevideo 4, 20144 ☎ 02 8372 8949 ◷ Mon–Fri lunch, dinner; Sat dinner only ⊖ Sant'Agostino

There's lots to see and do outside the restraints of the city; stroll the Navigli (canal) district, take in a game of soccer at the San Siro stadium, or in less than an hour you can be beside magical Lake Como.

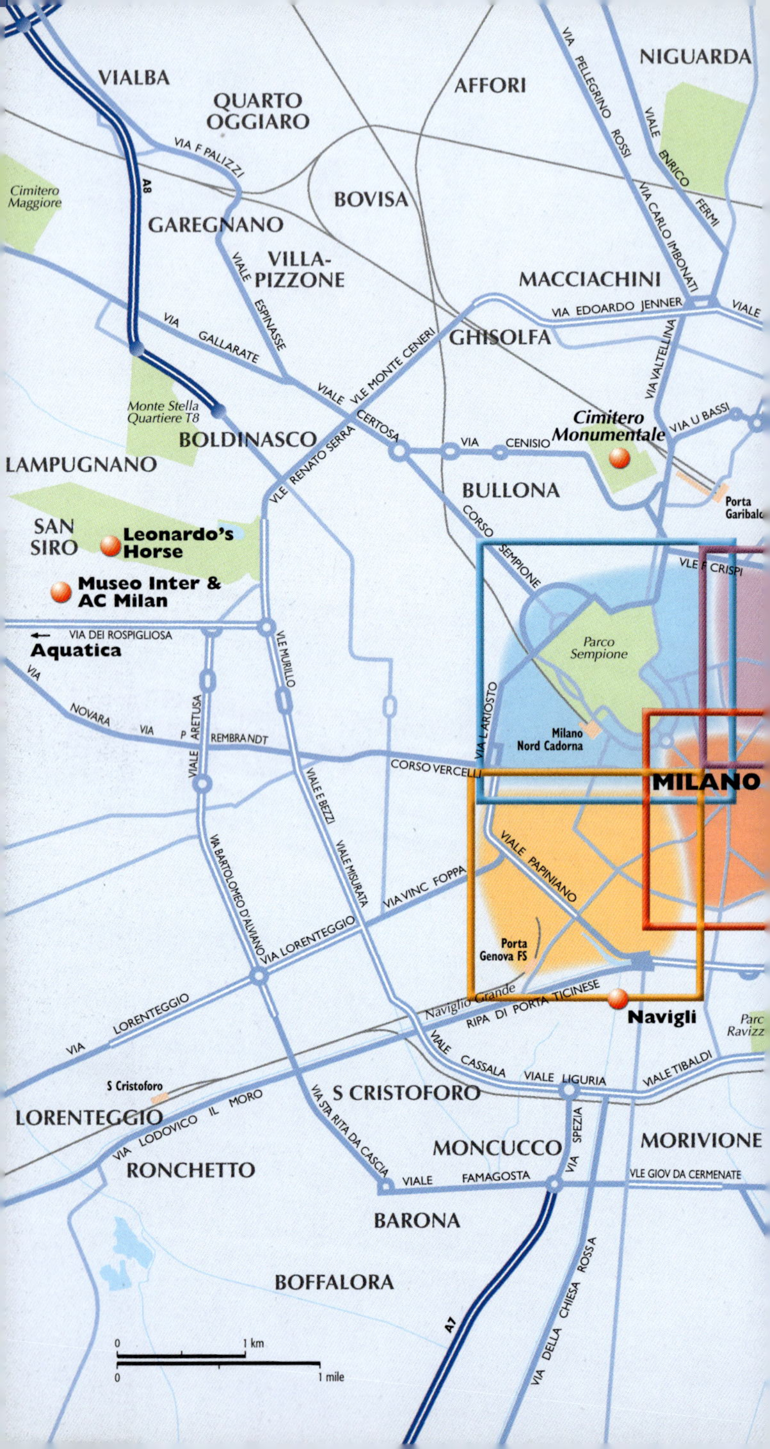

VIALBA
QUARTO OGGIARO
AFFORI
NIGUARDA
VIA F PALIZZI
VIA PELLEGRINO ROSSI
VIALE ENRICO FERMI
VIA CARLO IMBONATI
Cimitero Maggiore
A8
GAREGNANO
BOVISA
VILLA-PIZZONE
VIALE ESPINASSE
MACCIACHINI
VIA EDOARDO JENNER
VIALE
VIA GALLARATE
VLE MONTE CENERI
GHISOLFA
VIA VALTELLINA
VIA U BASSI
Monte Stella Quartiere T8
VLE RENATO SERRA
CERTOSA
VIA CENISIO
Cimitero Monumentale
BOLDINASCO
BULLONA
Porta Garibaldi
LAMPUGNANO
CORSO SEMPIONE
VLE F CRISPI
SAN SIRO
Leonardo's Horse
Museo Inter & AC Milan
Parco Sempione
VIA DEI ROSPIGLIOSA
Aquatica
VLE MURILLO
VIA L'ARIOSTO
Milano Nord Cadorna
MILANO
VIA NOVARA
VIA P ARETUSA
VIALE P ARETUSA
REMBRANDT
CORSO VERCELLI
VIALE E BEZZI
VIALE PAPINIANO
VIA BARTOLOMEO D'ALVIANO
VIALE MISURATA
VIA VINC FOPPA
VIA LORENTEGGIO
Porta Genova FS
Naviglio Grande
RIPA DI PORTA TICINESE
Navigli
Parc Ravizz
LORENTEGGIO
S Cristoforo
S CRISTOFORO
VIA LODOVICO IL MORO
VIA STA RITA DA CASCIA
VIALE CASSALA
VIALE LIGURIA
VIA SPEZIA
VIALE TIBALDI
MONCUCCO
MORIVIONE
RONCHETTO
VIALE FAMAGOSTA
VLE GIOV DA CERMENATE
BOFFALORA
BARONA
VIA DELLA CHIESA ROSSA
A7
0   1 km
0   1 mile

Farther Afield
PRATO CENTENARO
PRECOTTO
CRESCENZAGO
BICOCCA
SEGNANINO
SEGNANO
GRECO
GORLA
Naviglio della Martesana
VIALE FULVIO TESTI
MONZA
VIALE ZARA
VIALE
CIMIANO
VIA PALMANOVA
Lambro
TURRO
Parco Lambro
MARCHE
VIALE LUNIGIANA
VIALE BRIANZA
MONZA
VIALE
ROTTOLE
A51
V R LEONCAVALLO
VIALE
VIA ROMBON
ISOLA
VIA NICOLA ANTONIO PÓRPORA
Stazione Centrale
CORSO BUENOS AIRES
VIALE ABRUZZI
VIALE LOMBARDIA
Lambro
BAST DI PTA VENEZIA
Museo del Giocattolo e del Bambino
Giardini Pubblici
VIALE ROMAGNA
LAMBRATE
VIALE L MAJNO
VIALE DEI MILLE
ORTICA
Santa Maria della Passione
VIALE CAMPANIA
CORSO XXII MARZO
VIALE CORSICA
Giardino Guastella
Porta Vittoria
VIALE E CALDARA
VIALE UMBRIA
VIALE MOLISE
VIA MECENATE
CORSO LODI
Parco Alessandrini
VIALE ISONZO
CALVAIRATE
VIALE PUGLIE
LA TRECCIA
TALIEDO
VIA GIUSEPPE
CORSO LODI
RIPAMONTI
GAMBOLOITA
VIA B QUARANTA
VIA C MAROCHETTI V G CAV
MORSENCHIO
VIA VIRGILIO FERRARI
VIGENTINO
NOSEDO
AUTOSTRADA DEL SOLE
PONTINIA
ROGOREDO
A51
VAIANO VALLE

Navigli

Now being spruced up, the Navigli area is central to eating out and nightlife in the city

THE BASICS

✚ E8–F9

✉ Extends west of Piazza Maggio along Ripa di Porta Ticinese and south along Alzaia Naviglio Pavese

🚇 Porta Genova

🚌 59; tram 2, 3

♿ Accessible; some steps over bridges

HIGHLIGHTS

● Excellent selection of restaurants and bars
● Antiques market on last Sunday of each month
● Boat trips

Named for the navigable canals, this quarter of the city was once an important trade route for barges. Since barge transport ceased in 1979, the Navigli has gradually evolved into a popular arty and nightlife area.

Decades of neglect Don't expect pristine, picture-postcard canals; the area has undergone extensive renovation but still has room for more improvement. Until recently most money was invested in other parts of the city, the canals considered nothing but an eyesore, but now the potential has at long last been recognized. The murky waters have been dredged of debris, the towpaths rebuilt and the paving stones renewed. In winter the canals can be a disappointment, when they are drained and cleaned up ready for the summer, when it is possible to take a pleasurable two-hour boat tour.

Hive of industry The Navigli was once a working-class area with small artisan workshops lining the towpaths. With the increasing gentrification of the district and the rising costs of rents, these workshops have been pushed out to make way for shops, bars and restaurants—from old family-type *osterie* to sleek, trendy establishments.

After dark As the district develops, the back streets leading off from the canals are filling up with cocktail bars and disco-pubs, attracting a younger clientele. With continuing investment in the area, the Navigli is becoming the hippest place in town.

Santa Maria della Passione

Detail of the facade (left); Crespi's The Fasting of St. Charles *(right)*

The second-largest church in Milan after the Duomo, it is distinctive for its handsome dome. But the main attraction is the art within the church—a gallery of 16th- and 17th-century paintings and frescoes by leading Lombard artists.

Elaborate additions Santa Maria della Passione was built in the late 14th to early 15th centuries in a Greek cross plan and was extended with a nave and side chapels in 1573. The baroque facade, decorated with statues, was added in 1729 by Giuseppe Rusnati, who also built the adjoining convent, now the Conservatorio di Musica Giuseppe Verdi.

Artistic masterpieces The paintings and frescoes that decorate most of the church depict the Passion of Christ or similar themes. The paintings of saints perched on the piers of the nave are by Daniele Crespi. The church has numerous paintings by this Milanese master, considered the finest Lombard painter of the early 17th century. He died in his early 30s of the plague, but his output was considerable. In the first chapel on the left is Crespi's *Il Digiuno di San Carlo (The Fasting of St. Charles)*, which shows San Carlo Borromeo, Archbishop of Milan and mastermind of the Counter-Reformation. This is Crespi's best-known work and is generally regarded as the most famous 17th-century Milanese painting. It shows the saint with a loaf of bread and a carafe of water—a simple, austere composition reflecting the spirit of the Counter-Reformation.

THE BASICS

K5

Via Conservatorio 14, 20122

02 7602 1370

Mon–Sat 7.45–12, 3.30–5, Sun and holidays 9.30–12.30, 3.30–6.30. Limited opening during services

San Babila

54, 61

Good; one step

Free

If you have time, peek into the Giuseppe Verdi Conservatory of Music next door to the church to see the striking courtyard

HIGHLIGHTS

● Works by Daniele Crespi
● *The Last Supper* (1543), Gaudenzio Ferrari
● *Deposition* (1510), Bernardino Luini
● The church organs on either side of the choir, with beautiful 16th- and 17th-century carvings and shutters painted by Daniele Crespi

More to See

AQUATICA

www.parcoaquatica.com
A great family day out, this water park has pools, thrilling slides, fountains, tubes, river rides and artificial beaches.
✠ Off map at A3　✉ Via G Airaghi 61, 20153　☎ 02 4820 0134　🕔 Jun–Sep daily 9.30–6　🚇 De Angeli then bus 72, Primaticcio then bus 64, Lotto then bus 423　✋ Expensive

CIMITERO MONUMENTALE

The neo-Romanesque cemetery (1866) covers an area of 250,000sq m (900,000sq ft) in the northwest of the city. Eminent Milanese and other Italians, including novelist Manzoni and the poet Salvatore Quasimodo, are buried in the Famae Aedes (House of Fame). Fine sculpture.
✠ F1　✉ Piazzale Cimitero Monumentale, north end of Via Manzoni, 20154　☎ 02 8846 5600　🕔 Tue–Sat 8–6, Sun and holidays 8–1　🚌 37, 94; tram 2, 3, 12, 14, 33　♿ Good　✋ Free

GIARDINO GUASTALLA

The oldest public gardens in Milan, founded in 1555 by Paola Ludovica Torelli, Countess of Guastalla, who planned it as part of the Guastalla College for daughters of impoverished local nobles. There are several monuments and a fish pond.
✠ J7　✉ Via San Barnaba, 20122　🕔 Daily 7–7 (longer hours in summer)　🚌 60, 77; tram 12, 27

LEONARDO'S HORSE

The largest bronze equine statue in the world at 7m (24ft) high, this is a replica of a monument that Leonardo da Vinci was commissioned to build in 1482. It didn't get beyond model stage and was finally cast in 1999 in the US. It rather appropriately stands outside the horse-racing stadium, the Ippodrome (▷ 103) in San Siro.
✠ Off map at A2　✉ Piazzale dello Sport, San Siro 20151　🚇 Lotto　🚌 Tram 16

MUSEO DEL GIOCATTOLO E DEL BAMBINO

www.museodelgiocattolo.it
A huge toy museum about 3km (2 miles) east of the city. Displays include 18th-century toys, tin science-fiction

The majestic Leonardo's horse

toys and papier-maché dolls from the 1950s and 60s. Exhibits take on various themes, such as Pinocchio, the Golden Age of the Toy (1880–1915), Theater and Circus.

✚ Off map at M5 ✉ Via Pitteri 56, 20134 ☎ 02 2641 1585 🕐 Tue–Fri 9.30–4, Sat, Sun, public holidays 9.30–12.30, 3–6 🚇 Lambrate, then bus 75 ♿ Good ✋ Moderate

MUSEO INTER & AC MILAN

www.sansirotour.com

This museum is in the San Siro stadium, where both of Milan's soccer teams play. There are more than 3,000 items on display, including trophies, flags and memorabilia relating to Milan's two famous teams, Inter and AC. There are guided tours of the stadium every day except Sunday and when matches are in progress.

✚ Off map at A2 ✉ Stadio Giuseppe Meazza (San Siro), Gate 21, Via Piccolomini 5, 20151 ☎ 02 404 2432 🕐 Daily 9.30–6 (last entry 5); the museum is closed during sporting events 🚇 Lotto, then shuttle bus for matches or bus 49; tram 16 ♿ Good ✋ Expensive

PARCO LAMBRO

This large park (over 90ha/222 acres) to the east of the city is a good place to relax and escape the heat and noise of Milan in high summer. It was designed to mirror the natural Lombardy countryside with the River Lambro meandering through the middle and has numerous small lakes and ponds. Team sports and rowing are popular activities here.

✚ Off map at M1 🚇 Udine 🚌 55

STAZIONE CENTRALE

www.milanocentrale.it

Majestic Stazione Centrale is not just Milan's main railway station but is the biggest in all Italy. Although it was not completed until 1931, it was designed in 1912 and its style is more characteristic of art nouveau than the heavy Fascist architecture of the 1930s.

✚ K1 ✉ Piazzale Duca d'Aosta, 20124 ☎ 02 7252 4360 🕐 24 hours, tourist information Mon–Sat 9–6.30, Sun 9–12.30, 1.30–6 🚇 Centrale 🚌 42, 60, 82, 92; tram 2, 5, 33 ✋ Good

Get away from it all in the attractive Parco Lambro

Excursions

Distance: 48km (30 miles)
Journey time: 1 hour
🚆 Regular service from Garibaldi FS
ℹ️ Via Gombito 13
☎ 035 242 226;
www.apt.bergamo.it

BERGAMO

Northeast of Milan in the southern foothills of the Alps, Bergamo could not be more different from Italy's business capital.

Remarkably unspoiled, historic Bergamo crowns a steep hill. The city is divided into the medieval Città Alta (Upper Town), within 16th-century walls, and the contrasting modern, traffic-filled Città Bassa (Lower Town). A funicular transports you to Città Alta and its picturesque cobbled alleyways and medieval and Renaissance buildings. Visit Piazza del Duomo, where the Duomo pales against the Renaissance porch of the Basilica of Santa Maria Maggiore and lavish facade of the Cappella Colleoni. The highlight of the lower town is the Galleria Accademia Carrara and its collection of Venetian, Bergamesque and other works of art.

Distance: 93km (58 miles)
Journey time: 2 hours
🚆 Regular service from Stazione Centrale
ℹ️ Piazza del Comune 5
☎ 0372 23233;
www.aptcremona.it

CREMONA

A quiet market town on the banks of the River Po, Cremona has been the heart of the violin-making industry since 1566.

The greatest violin maker, Antonio Stradivari, was born here in 1644, and is commemorated in the Museo Stradivariano, where many of his tools are on display. In the middle of town is Piazza del Comune, a fine medieval square with beautiful medieval monuments: the highest bell tower in Italy, the Romanesque/Gothic cathedral, the octagonal Baptistry (1167) and the Palazzo del Comune (1206–45). The Palazzo del Comune has a collection of historic violins, including examples by Amati and Stradivari.

LAKE COMO

Its temperate climate and lavish villas make Como the most romantic of the three major Italian lakes. Enjoy boating trips, walks in the mountains, visits to lakeshore villas and wonderful views.

Surrounded by high mountains and rugged hills, Lake Como has inspired writers, artists and musicians from Pliny the Younger in Roman times to 19th-century Romantics such as French novelists Stendhal and Flaubert. Today it also draws celebrities. The first steamboat was launched from here in 1826 and visitors have been taking boat trips to enjoy the views of lakeside ever since. Como is smaller than Lake Maggiore and Garda but it has the longest perimeter (over 170km/106 miles) and at its deepest point, between Argegno and Nesso, it measures 410m (1,345ft), making it the deepest lake in Italy.

THE BASICS

Distance: 50km (31 miles)
Journey time: 30 min to hour depending on departure station

Regular service from Stazione Centrale to Como town (30 min); Cardorna (1 hour)

Piazza Cavour 17, 22100 Como ☎ 031 269712; www.lakecomo.com

PAVIA

Pavia is graced by fine Romanesque and medieval buildings, but what really draws the crowds is the nearby 14th-century monastery.

Certosa di Pavia (8km/5 miles north of Pavia) is one of the most extravagant religious complexes in Northern Italy—the exuberant facade in multitoned marble has a wealth of inlay and sculpture. Inside there is a profusion of Renaissance and baroque art. Pavia's rich heritage of art and architecture is reflected in its Renaissance cathedral, whose architects include Leonardo da Vinci, Bramante and Amadeo, several fine medieval churches and the Visconti castle.

THE BASICS

Distance: 39km (24 miles)
Journey time: 45 min

Service from Stazione Centrale to Famagosta station, then 15-min walk

Piazza Petrarca 4 ☎ 0382 595001; www.provincia.pv.it

PROFUMERIA
aline

AC MILAN AND INTER

www.acmilan.com; www.inter.it
Catch one of Italy's top soccer clubs, AC Milan or Inter, at the San Siro on alternate weekends during the season. Tickets for matches sell out fast, so it is best to buy in advance on the website or, for Inter, from branches of Banca Popolare di Milano, for AC, from branches of Cariplo bank.
➕ Off map at A2 ✉ Via Piccolomini 5, 20151 🕓 Sep–Jun 🚇 Lotto then free bus before matches 🚌 Tram 16

ALCATRAZ

www.alcatrazmilano.com
Rock-oriented live music and disco venue frequented by the occasional famous face.
➕ Off map at G1 ✉ Via Valtellina 25, 20121 ☎ 02 6901 6352 🚇 Garibaldi

AUDITORIUM DI MILANO

www.laverdi.org
A multipurpose hall and the home of the Orchestra Sinfonica di Milano Giuseppe Verdi. Symphony concerts, choral works and chamber music; also jazz and light music.
➕ Off map at F9 ✉ Largo G Mahler, 20136 ☎ 02 8338 9401/2/3 🚇 Romolo, then trolley bus 90, 91 🚌 59, 71

BLUE NOTE

www.bluenotemilano.com
Perfect venue for listening to top-quality international jazz. Also a restaurant and a bar. You get the chance to catch some big international names.
➕ Off map at G1 ✉ Via Borsieri 37, 20159 ☎ 02 690 1688 🚇 Garibaldi

CENTRO SPORTIVO MARIO SAINI

This tennis facility has an open-air clay court and 12 indoor synthetic courts. Equipment is available to rent. Non-members welcome, but tennis whites are appreciated.
➕ Off map at M4 ✉ Via Corelli 136, 20134 ☎ 02 756 2741 🕓 Mon–Sat dawn–dusk 🚌 38

MEAZZA STADIUM

Renamed after Giuseppe Meazza, one of Italy's all-time great soccer players, in 1980, this famous stadium is more commonly called San Siro, after the district surrounding it. A remarkable design: the building gives the impression that it is wrapped up by the spiraling access flights. It was originally built in 1926 as a gift from Piero Pirelli, the then-president of AC Milan, and could only seat 10,000. A second tier was added in 1955 and a third plus a fiberglass roof supported by 12 cylindrical concrete towers was added in 1987, making the stadium's capacity over 85,000. The 1990 World Cup was staged at San Siro.

COLOSSEO

There is a choice of three screens, called the Visconti, Allen and Chaplin—all names with movie connections—plus a bar.
➕ B8 ✉ Viale Monte Nero 84, 20135 ☎ 02 5990 1361 🚇 Porta Romano

DUCALE MULTISALA

www.cinenauta.it
The Ducale has been converted from an old cinema into a modern four-screen movie house with a pleasant bar.
➕ B8 ✉ Piazza Napoli 27, 20146 ☎ 199 208 002 🚇 Porta Genova

GOLF CLUB MILANO

www.golfclubmilano.it
This prestigious 18-hole golf course 30 minutes from Milan is close to the town of Monza. Pro shop, driving range, pool and restaurant.
➕ Off map to north ✉ Viale Mulini San Giorgio 7, 20052 Monza ☎ 039 303 081

IPPODROME DEL GALOPPO/TROTTING

www.trenno.it
For horseracing fans there is a full calendar of flat racing events from March to November. In the separate arena across the road, trotting races take place throughout the year, except for the month of August.
➕ Off map at A2 ✉ Piazzale dello Sport, San Siro 20151 ☎ 02 482 161 🚇 Lotto 🚌 Tram 16

MAGAZZINI GENERALI

www.magazzinigenerali.it
A mixed crowd works up a sweat grooving to a good range of music at this nightclub, spread over two floors.
✚ Off map at J9 ✉ Via Pietrasanta 14, 20141 ☎ 02 539 3948 Ⓜ Lodi Tibb

PLASTIC

With four bars and three music rooms, this club, which has been dancing for 25 years, is one of the best in Milan.
✚ M7 ✉ Viale Umbria 120, 20131 ☎ 02 733 996 Ⓜ 92; Tram 12

PLINIUS

www.multisalaplinius.com
Six screens showing the latest mainstream films.
✚ M2 ✉ Viale Abruzzi 28–30, 20131 ☎ 02 2953 1103 Ⓜ Loreto, Lima

POGUE MAHONE

If you require a night away from the typical Italian bar—to drink Guinness and watch soccer, for example—head for this popular Irish pub. Live bands.
✚ K8 ✉ Via Salmini 1, 20135 ☎ 02 5830 9726 Ⓜ Porta Romana

ROLLING STONE

www.rollingstone.it
Listen to live rock, punk, indie and jazz at this relaxed hangout.
✚ L6 ✉ Corso XXII Marzo 32, 20135 ☎ 02 733172 Ⓜ Porta Vittorio

LE ROVEDINE

www.rovedine.com
Milan's only public golf course lies 6km (4 miles) outside the city.
✚ Off map to east ✉ Via Karl Marx 18, Noverasco di Opera, 20090 ☎ 02 5760 6420

TEATRO CARCANO

www.teatrocarcano.com
First opened to the public in 1803, the theater underwent major changes in the 1980s. Theatrical productions include staged versions of films, and it is also used for lectures by the university.
✚ J7 ✉ Corso di Porta Romana 63, 20122 ☎ 02 5518 1362/5518 1377 Ⓜ Crocetta

TEATRO CIAK

A popular venue for a variety of performance styles, including comedy, cabaret and murder mystery plays. A great place

ITALIAN GRAND PRIX

The Italian Grand Prix at Monza ranks alongside Monte Carlo as one of the glitziest Grands Prix on the Formula 1 circuit. Plenty of stars and models watch the race under a sea of red Ferrari flags. Ticket information can be found on the website.
✚ Off map to north ✉ Parco di Monza, 20052 Monza ☎ 039 248 2212; www.monzanet.it Ⓢ Sep Ⓡ From Stazione Centrale

to spot emerging talent. Reserve in advance.
✚ Off map at M4 ✉ Via Sangallo 33, 20133 ☎ 02 7611 0093 Ⓜ Dateo Ⓡ Tram 5

TRANSILVANIA

www.transilvanialive.it
There is more of a youthful feel than most rock clubs at this extremely noisy venue, a hot spot for visiting rockers. Details of live bands are on the website.
✚ Off map at A4 ✉ Via Paravia 59, 20148 ☎ 02 4871 2578 Ⓜ Bande Nere, then bus 95

TROPICANA CLUB LATINO

www.tropicanamilano.it
The place to go for Latin-American dancing. The mostly over-30s crowd move to the rhythm of salsa and tango over three floors.
✚ H8 ✉ Viale Bligny 52, 20136 ☎ 02 5843 6525 Ⓜ Porta Romana

TUNNEL CLUB

www.tunnel-milano.it
An unusual space created in a converted warehouse under the central station. A variety of live music, DJ evenings, poetry readings, film shows and exhibitions, and you can enjoy cocktails at the bar. Prices are lower than other more conventional venues in the city.
✚ K1 ✉ Via Sammartini 30, 20125 ☎ 02 6671 1370 Ⓜ Centrale FS

PRICES

Prices are approximate, based on a 3-course meal for one person.

€€€   over €50
€€   €20–€50
€   under €20

ACQUASALA (€€)

www.acquasala.it
Quickly establishing itself as one of Milan's top restaurants, the cooking celebrates Pugliese cuisine, served in refined surroundings.
E8 ⊠ Ripa di Porta Ticinese 71, 20143 ☎ 02 8942 3989 Tue–Sun lunch, dinner Porta Genova

AIMO E NADIA (€€€)

www.aimoenadia.com
Central Italian cuisine, cooked by award-winning chef Signor Aimo and his wife, Nadia. Every dish is a masterpiece, served in intimate surroundings. Tempts the senses of sight, smell and taste.
Off map A7 ⊠ Via Montecuccoli 6, 20146 ☎ 02 416 886 Mon–Fri lunch, dinner; Sat dinner only Primaticcio

AL PONT DE FERR (€–€€)

www.pontdeferr.it
Traditional *osteria* with brick archways and wood panels. Try the vegetable crêpes with cheese.
E8 ⊠ Ripa di Porta Ticinese 55, 20143 ☎ 02 8940 6277 Tue–Sun lunch, dinner Porta Genova

ASSO DI FIORI (€€)

www.assodifiori.com
Attractive traditional restaurant by the canal, dedicated to cheese, cheese and more cheese! But delicious desserts, too.
E8 ⊠ Alzaia Naviglio Grande 54, 20144 ☎ 02 8940 9415 Mon–Sat lunch, dinner; Sun dinner only Porta Genova

ATLAS FOYER (€€–€€€)

The place to be seen with the glitterati, this remake of an old movie theater has retained the art nouveau embellishments.
Off map L3 ⊠ Via Sansovino 1, 20133 ☎ 02 2024 2298 Dinner daily Piola

BE BOP (€€)

Elegant pizza and pasta restaurant, where cooking

is also directed at vegetarians and coeliacs—90 percent of the menu is gluten free.
G8 ⊠ Viale Col di Lana 4, 20136 ☎ 02 837 6972 Lunch, dinner Porta Genova Tram 3

LA BOTTEGA DEL GELATO (€€)

www.labottegadelgelato.it
This *gelateria*, not far from the central station, has been in business since the mid-19th century. Delicious ice cream, including peach, passion fruit, melon and tamarillo.
L2 ⊠ Via Pergolesi 3, 20124 ☎ 02 2940 0076 Thu–Tue Caiazzo

LA COZZERIA (€)

www.lacozzeria.it
Each dish here is based upon a kilogram (about 2lb) of mussels. Chefs curry them, pepper them, make them into a soup or serve them with cream, spices or liqueurs.
L8 ⊠ Via Muratori 6, 20135 ☎ 02 5410 7164 Tue–Sun lunch, dinner Porta Romana

DA GASPARE (€€)

www.ristorantedagaspare.com
Despite refreshingly low prices, Da Gaspare stands head and shoulders above the rest of Milan's fish restaurants. Lobster, mussels, crab and more crustaceans. Tasty desserts, too. Small, uncomfortable and often noisy, but the regulars keep flooding back.

✚ B5 ✉ Via Carlo Ravizza 19 20149 ☎ 02 4800 6409 🕙 Thu–Tue lunch, dinner Ⓜ Buonarroti

EL BRELLÍN (€€)

www.brellin.com
Atmospheric restaurant in an attractive former grocery and washhouse beside the canal. Typical Milanese cooking and good wine list. Try the Sunday brunch.
✚ E8 ✉ Alzaia Naviglio Grande 14, 20144 ☎ 02 5810 1351 🕙 Mon–Sat lunch, dinner; Sun brunch only Ⓜ Porta Genova

IL GIORNO BISTROT (€€)

www.hotelhermitagemilano.com
In the elegant Hermitage Hotel, north of the city, this smart dining room gives traditional northern Italian cuisine a contemporary twist. Good choice for those who prefer gluten-free food.
✚ E2 ✉ Via Messina 10, 20154 ☎ 02 318 170 🕙 Mon–Sat lunch, dinner Ⓜ Garibaldi 🚍 Tram 14

L'OLANDESE VOLANTE (€€€)

A ship theme complete with fishing nets draped on the walls is an ideal backdrop for the fine fish dishes served here. The day's catch is displayed in a cabinet.
✚ E8 ✉ Via Argelati 1, 20121 ☎ 02 8941 5892 🕙 Tue–Sun lunch, dinner Ⓜ Porta Genova

ORSI (€€)

This *gelateria* down by the canal wins in summer with its nice terrace. The variety of flavors is impressive—blueberry and zabaglione to name just two.
✚ F9 ✉ Via Torricelli 19, 20136 ☎ 02 8940 6807 🕙 Tue–Sun Ⓜ Romolo

PONTE ROSSO (€€)

www.trattoriaponterosso.it
Not your typical trattoria—this one is smart with a trendy orange and black interior, and looks more like a French bistro. Home-cooked Italian food like *mamma* used to make.
✚ E8 ✉ Ripa di Porta Ticinese 23, 20143 ☎ 02 837 3132 🕙 Tue–Sat lunch, dinner; Mon dinner only Ⓜ Porta Genova

---

IL CONTO

The bill (check), *il conto*, usually includes extras such as *servizio* (service). Iniquitous cover charges (*pane e coperto*) have now been outlawed, but some restaurants still try to get round the regulations. Only pay for bread (*pane*) if you have asked for it. Proper receipts—not a scrawled piece of paper—must be given by law. If you receive a scrap of paper, which is more likely in a pizzeria, and have doubts about the total, ask for a proper receipt (*una fattura* or *una ricevuta*).

IL SOLITO POSTO (€€)

www.ilsolitoposto.net
Since 1888 this trattoria has been serving happy customers in the heart of Como, a few steps from the lake shore. Dishes are lovingly prepared and delicious. The carpaccio is superb and the restaurant is known for its *osso bucco*.
✚ Off map ✉ Via Lambertenghi 9, 22100 Como ☎ 031 271 352 🕙 Daily 12–3, 7–11.15 🚆 From Milano Centrale

TRATTORIA TRE TORRI (€€)

The trip to Bergamo would be worth it just to dine in this trattoria in the heart of the walled medieval fortress high above the city. In the summer, savor beautifully prepared local cuisine in the garden. Don't miss the polenta with porcini mushrooms and taleggio cheese.
✚ Off map ✉ Piazza Mercato del Fieno 7/A, 24129 Bergamo ☎ 035 244 474 🕙 Daily lunch and dinner 🚆 From Milano Centrale, then funicular to old town

LE VIGNE (€€)

There is a lot of hustle and bustle at this rustic *osteria* on the canalside. It does get very crowded but the food is worth waiting for, especially the stews.
✚ E8 ✉ Ripa di Porta Ticinese 61, 20143 ☎ 02 5811 3224 🕙 Mon–Sat lunch, dinner Ⓜ Porta Genova

There is a wide range of accommodations in Milan. Choose from world-class deluxe hotels in historic buildings, chic boutique hotels or family-run smaller hotels that haven't changed much in 30 years.

Introduction

You'll find the full range of hotel options in Milan as you would in any prosperous city. Prices can be steep, as establishments in the upper price range outnumber inexpensive options.

Best to Book

Although Milan has plenty of accommodations, the city is a major commercial hub with a constant flow of businesspeople, so you will need to book in advance—especially if there is a trade fair or fashion show taking place at the same time. As there tend to be more commercial visitors than tourists, Milan's hotels are usually more in demand during the week, leaving more rooms available on weekends, when hotels may drop their prices. As a large proportion of the hotels are located in clusters on the perimeter areas around the city, it can be difficult to secure a place to stay right in the *centro* without paying high prices.

Saving Money

Agree on a price before you make your reservation. Hotels often quote their most expensive price: ask if they have a cheaper room available. Sometimes they offer reduced weekend rates. Smaller hotels can be open to gentle bargaining, particularly during quieter times. Some hotels are willing to put another bed in a room for an extra 35 per cent, ideal for families. Rates vary according to season, sometimes as much as 25 per cent, and increase dramatically when there are trade events taking place.

TIPS

● If you haven't booked in advance, the local visitor information office will have lists and may be willing to make reservations for you.

● It's perfectly acceptable to ask to see the room before you decide to stay somewhere.

● You will usually have to show your passport at check-in, as hotels are required to collect guest details.

● Check-out time is normally 11am–12, but hotels will usually store your luggage till the end of the day.

All the comforts and modern facilities can be found in Milanese hotels

PRICES

Expect to pay under €160 per night for a double room in a budget hotel.

HOSTEL VERONA

www.hostelveronamilan.com
Near Stazione Centrale, Hostel Verona makes a good-value base for exploring Milan. The 19 small whitewashed rooms are spartan, but have televisions and phones—some have a private bathroom.

✚ J2 ✉ Via Carlo Tenca 12, 20124 ☎ 02 6698 3091 Ⓜ Repubblica

HOTEL CASA MIA

www.casamiahotel.it
This is a good choice if your budget does not stretch to a four-star. It is in a decent location close to the metro, with very friendly, helpful staff and the 15 rooms are extremely clean.

✚ J3 ✉ Viale Vittorio Veneto 30, 20124 ☎ 02 657 5249 Ⓜ Repubblica

HOTEL DUE GIARDINI

www.hotelduegiardini.it
Excellent value hotel near Stazione Centrale. No elevator but staff are on hand to help with luggage. All rooms have modern comforts and private bathrooms. Breakfast is served in the garden when weather permits.

✚ K2 ✉ Via Benedetto Marcello 47, 20124 ☎ 02 2952 1093 Ⓜ Centrale FS

HOTEL NUOVO

www.hotelnuovomilano.com
Good value for a central spot. All 36 rooms are clean and compact—most have telephone, TV and, some, a private bathroom. Can be noisy at night.

✚ H6 ✉ Piazza Beccaria Cesare 6, 20122 ☎ 02 8646 4444 Ⓜ San Babila

IDEA HOTEL MILANO CORSO GENOVA

www.ideahotel.it
On a quiet green side street not far from the Navigli canals, this modern hotel offers simple, good quality and contemporary-bedrooms; some have a view of the Duomo.

✚ F7 ✉ Via Conca del Naviglio 20, 20123 ☎ 02 3666 82 333 Ⓜ Sant'Ambrogio

LONDON HOTEL

www.hotel-london-milan.com
You get a warm welcome

at this central hotel, where the comfy lounge is a popular place to gather. Overlooking a tranquil back street, the 30 large rooms are spartan and slightly dated.

✚ G5 ✉ Via Rovello 3, 20121 ☎ 02 7202 0166 Ⓜ Cairoli

ROVELLO

www.hotel-rovello.it
Intimate hotel with just 10 rooms, midway between the Duomo and Parco Sempione. Full of character, the rooms have wooden floors and beams, and overlook a courtyard.

✚ G5 ✉ Via Rovello 18, 20121 ☎ 02 8646 4654 Ⓜ Cairoli

SAN FRANCISCO

www.hotel-sanfrancisco.it/sito/
This family-run hotel close to the Giardini Pubblici has 31 simple rooms and a small, beautiful garden. Warm and welcoming staff.

✚ Off map at M1 ✉ Viale Lombardia 55, 20131 ☎ 02 236 0302 Ⓜ Piola

SPERONARI

A short walk from Galleria Vittorio Emanuele. The 24 rooms are small and basic but clean and tidy—some have a private bathroom. You will find that during trade fairs the hotel fills up with business guests.

✚ G6 ✉ Via Speronari 4, 20123 ☎ 02 8646 1125 Ⓜ Duomo

Mid-Range Hotels

PRICES

Expect to pay between €160 and €350 per night for a double room in a mid-range hotel.

ANTICA LOCANDA LEONARDO

www.anticalocandaleonardo.com

Comfort and refinement in a peaceful atmosphere. The 20 rooms have been renovated, and are tastefully furnished, from an authentic antique style to a more classic style, while the walls are adorned with works of art by contemporary artists. During good weather, take advantage of the pretty internal garden.

✠ E5 ✉ Corso Magenta 78, 20123 ☎ 02 4801 4197 Ⓜ Cadorna

ANTICA LOCANDA SOLFERINO

www.anticalocandasolferino.it

Tucked away in a quiet cobbled street, this delightful old-fashioned *pensione* is very friendly. The simple but spacious rooms, decorated with antiques, have pretty balconies. There are only 11 rooms, so book in advance.

✠ H3 ✉ Via Castelfidardo 2, 20121 ☎ 02 657 0129 Ⓜ Moscova

BAVIERA

www.hotelbaviera.com

Comfortable if slightly behind the times, this extremely gracious hotel considers itself a business person's hotel. A pleasant, updated lounge has restful sofas and wooden floors. The 50 bedrooms vary in size and have old-fashioned bedding. Within walking distance of Stazione Centrale.

✠ K3 ✉ Via Castaldi 7, 20124 ☎ 02 659 0551 Ⓜ Repubblica

BRISTOL

www.hotelbristolmil.it

Exit the Milano Centrale station via the stairs and you'll find yourself at the front door of this classic hotel. A refined Anglo-French style blends with modern amenities, which

PRICES

Italian hotels charge for the room not for each person. The price, by law, should be displayed in the room itself and may or may not include breakfast. Prices for different rooms often vary within a hotel, so if a room is too expensive be sure to ask if another is available for less (you may well be shown the most expensive first). Single rooms are in short supply and can cost nearly as much as a double room. Hotels in Milan are expensive, but they are generally of a good standard. It is best to book well in advance, particularly if there is a fashion show or trade fair taking place at the time.

include 68 soundproofed rooms and in-room Jacuzzis and Internet facilities. Helpful English-speaking staff.

✠ K1 ✉ Via Scarlatti 32, 20124 ☎ 02 669 4141 Ⓜ Repubblica

CANADA

www.canadahotel.it

What this glass structure lacks in character it makes up for with 35 pristine, modern rooms that will meet all your needs. There are good views of the Duomo from the eighth floor. About a 10-minute walk from the *centro storico*.

✠ H7 ✉ Via Santa Sofia 16, 20122 ☎ 02 5830 4844 Ⓜ Crocetta

CARLYLE BRERA

www.carlylebrerahotel.com

The stylish Carlyle Brera, in the Brera district, is a cut above most business hotels. It provides free bicycles to use around town and a high-class buffet breakfast. Very near to the metro station. 94 rooms.

✠ G3 ✉ Corso Garibaldi 84, 20121 ☎ 02 2900 3888 Ⓜ Moscova

CAVOUR

www.hotelcavour.it

In an ideal spot between La Scala and the Giardini Pubblici, this friendly hotel's 113 large rooms are decorated in cream with light-wood panels and have satellite TV and air-conditioning.

✚ H4 ✉ Via Fatebenefratelli 21, 20121 ☎ 02 620 001 Ⓜ Turati

GRAN DUCA DI YORK

www.ducadiyork.com
Housed in a grand 18th-century building, within a short distance of Piazza Duomo and the Pinacoteca Ambrosiana. The 33 standard rooms are plain but comfortable and soundproofed. There are superior rooms available; ask for one of the four rooms with a terrace.
✚ G6 ✉ Via Moneta 1, 20123 ☎ 02 874 863 Ⓜ Cordusio

HOTEL MICHELANGELO

www.michelangelohotelmilan.com
Convenient for transport to Milan's two major airports as Stazione Centrale is visible from the hotel. Many of the 300 bedrooms have a Jacuzzi and other mod cons, all surrounded by a gleaming wooden finish.
✚ K1 ✉ Via Scarlatti 33, 20124 ☎ 02 67551 Ⓜ Centrale FS

KING

www.hotelkingmilano.com
Housed in a lovely *palazzo* in a lively central spot, this pleasant hotel has an opulent lobby with period furniture, 48 comfortable rooms and efficient, courteous staff.
✚ F5 ✉ Via Corso Magenta 19, 20123 ☎ 02 874 432 Ⓜ Cadorna

UNA MAISON MILANO

www.unamaisonmilano.com
The 27 newly redesigned and well-appointed rooms in this attractive hotel include 11 suites, and are well designed for extended stays and business travelers. The Duomo is less than a five-minute walk from the door.
✚ G6 ✉ Via Mazzini 4, 20123 ☎ 02 85605 Ⓜ Duomo

MANIN

www.hotelmanin.it
A sophisticated, modern hotel on the edge of the prestigious shopping streets and opposite Giardini Pubblici. The huge conservatory-garden area is ideal for lunch or a cocktail. Nicely decorated throughout, with 118 spacious bedrooms;

some with terrace or balcony overlooking the gardens.
✚ J3 ✉ Via Manin 7, 20121 ☎ 02 659 6511 Ⓜ Turati

MANZONI

www.hotelmanzoni.com
After an overhaul in 2007, this hotel is an elegant and comfortable place to stay. On a quiet street yet still in a central location. The 45 rooms are well appointed and there is a wellness complex. Falls at the top end of the mid-range category.
✚ H5 ✉ Via Santo Spirito 20, 20124 ☎ 02 7600 5700 Ⓜ Montenapoleone

REGINA

www.hotelregina.it
A charming 18th-century mansion adorned with antique furniture and paintings. The 43 rooms have an old-fashioned appeal, with parquet floors and large rugs. Near the Navigli canals. Pretty garden.
✚ F7 ✉ Via Cesare Correnti 13, 20123 ☎ 02 5810 6913 Ⓜ Missori

SPADARI AL DUOMO

www.spadarihotel.com
A small hotel with contemporary art and sculpture displayed against vivid blue decoration. The 39 spacious bedrooms have designer furniture. No restaurant, but snacks are served. A few steps from Teatro alla Scala.
✚ G6 ✉ Via Spadari 11, 20123 ☎ 02 7200 2371 Ⓜ Duomo

Luxury Hotels

PRICES

Expect to pay over €350 per night for a double room in a luxury hotel.

FOUR SEASONS

www.fourseasons.com/milan
A beautifully restored 15th-century monastery in the Quad d'Oro set around a cloistered court-yard. The huge opulent reception has frescoes, columns and vaults, and the 118 spacious bed-rooms are stylish.
✚ H5 ✉ Via Gesù 6/8, 21021 ☎ 02 77088 Ⓜ Montenapoleone

GRAND HOTEL ET DE MILAN

www.grandhoteletdemilan.it
The Grand has an envi-able position, right next door to La Scala. For 150 years the Grand has opened its doors to royals and celebrities. The hotel oozes distinction, with staff buzzing around the ornate foyer catering to guests' every need. The 77 rooms have period decoration, yet the hotel's facilities are firmly 21st century, including a fit-ness area.
✚ H4 ✉ Via Manzoni 29, 20121 ☎ 02 723 141 Ⓜ Montenapoleone

THE GRAY

www.hotelthegray.com
Facing the renowned Galleria, this stylish hotel is minimalist design at its best: dim lighting and metallic decoration with a splash of red. Framed prints and modern lights enhance the 21 rooms, all with the latest mod cons including DVDs and hydro tubs.
✚ H5 ✉ Via San Raffaele 6, 20121 ☎ 02 720 8951 Ⓜ Duomo

HERMITAGE

www.hotelhermitagemilano.com
A refined hotel out near the Cimitero Monumentale with 131 bright, spacious rooms, all furnished in dark wood. Il Giorno Bistrot restaurant is said to be one of the best in Milan (▷ 106).
✚ E2 ✉ Via Messina 10, 20154 ☎ 02 318 170 Ⓜ Garibaldi

PRINCIPE DI SAVOIA

www.dorchestercollection.com
Meticulous gardens lead-ing up to a majestic white facade give an indication of the sumptuous interior you are about to enter. With a 1930s feel, the rooms are adorned with antiques, marble and luxury carpets. The 401 (269 rooms and 132 suites) are a generous size. Indoor pool and fit-ness and beauty complex.
✚ J3 ✉ Piazza della Repubblica 17, 20124 ☎ 02 62301 Ⓜ Repubblica

SHERATON DIANA MAJESTIC

www.sheratondianamajestic.com
Set in pretty gardens, close to Milan's main shopping area, this art deco hotel is the place to be seen; it is popular during fashion shows with models and journalists. The circular foyer has leather chairs and period furniture, and the 107 Imperial-style rooms have elegant marble bathrooms.
✚ K4 ✉ Viale Piave 42, 20129 ☎ 02 20581 Ⓜ Porta Venezia

STRAF

www.straf.it
Unconventional modern comfort in a prime spot next to the Duomo. An ultra-sleek minimalist look has been created using materials such as raw con-crete, iron, slate, burnished brass, gauze-effect glass and scratched mirrors. 64 rooms.
✚ H5 ✉ Via San Raffaele 3, 20121 ☎ 02 805 081 Ⓜ Duomo

HOTEL GRADING

Italian hotels, including those in Milan, are classified by the state system into five categories, from one to five stars. As this is based entirely on facilities offered, it could mean a charmingly furnished atmospheric two-star *pensione* may cost less than a run-down three-star business hotel. This is further compli-cated by a fewer-stars-less-tax situation, with some hoteliers happy not to upgrade themselves.

Use this section to help you plan your visit to Milan. You will find information about getting around once you are there, as well as useful tips and a language section.

Planning Ahead

When to Go

Milan is primarily a business destination, with little seasonal variation in the number of visitors or cost of hotels, but avoid visiting during major events, such as fashion shows. April, May, June and September are good months to visit. June begins to get hot and it cools off at the end of September when there are increasing bouts of rain.

TIME

Italy is one hour ahead of GMT, six hours ahead of New York and nine hours ahead of Los Angeles.

AVERAGE DAILY MAXIMUM TEMPERATURES

JAN	FEB	MAR	APR	MAY	JUN	JUL	AUG	SEP	OCT	NOV	DEC
43°F	46°F	54°F	59°F	68°F	73°F	79°F	79°F	70°F	61°F	54°F	45°F
6°C	8°C	12°C	15°C	20°C	23°C	26°C	26°C	21°C	16°C	12°C	7°C

Spring (March to May) is very pleasant, although rain can persist into May.

Summer (June to August) high temperatures bring a humid haze and normally some thunderstorms, which help to clear the air.

Autumn (September to November) gradually turns from showers to heavy rain, and November is dank and wet.

Winter (December to February) Alpine winds make it very cold and there can be heavy frosts and thick fog. December can produce pleasant bright, crisp days.

WHAT'S ON

January *Corteo dei Re Magi* (6 Jan): A Nativity-theme procession travels from the Duomo to Sant'Eustorgio.

February *Carnevale Ambrosiano*: The carnival culminates with a parade on the first Saturday of Lent.

March MODIT-*Milanovendemodo* (early Mar): International fashion show.

Milano–San Remo (third Sat): Milan hosts the start of this famous international bicycle race.

April *Fiera dei Fiori* (Mon after Easter): Fair devoted to flower growing, near Sant' Angelo Franciscan convent.

Stramilano (early Apr): Annual marathon race with over 50,000 competitors.

June *Festa del Naviglio* (first Sun): Festival held along the Navigli canals; concerts, street performers, sports, handicrafts and regional cooking.

July/August *Festival Latino-Americano*: Festival of Latin-American music, handicrafts and cuisine.

September *Gran Premio di Monza*: Formula One Grand Prix of Italy.

October MODIT-*Milanovendemoda* (early Oct): second major fashion show.

December *Festa di Sant'Ambrogio* (4–7 Dec): Festival celebrating Sant'Ambrogio, Milan's fourth-century patron saint and the city's first mayor. Stalls are set up around the Sforza Castle exterior walls and most people take the day off work to attend the market. Also called *Oh Bej! Oh Bej!* after the children's cries of delight in the 16th century.

Milan Online

www.turismo.comune.milano.it
Milan's city website includes practical information on city sights, restaurants, nightlife, shopping, transport and practical information.

www.provincia.milano.it/turismo
The tourist office website is in English and has general information on the city sights. Also good information on accessiblity.

www.hellomilano.it
English site that is easy to understand and has good up-to-date details on what's on, news, restaurants, nightlife, shopping and general information.

www.enit.it
The main Italian Tourist Board website carries a wealth of information about the whole country—available in several languages.

www.emmeti.it
An Italy-based site, in English and Italian, with a good range of information on Milan and links to other sites. It's strong on local events and offers an online hotel booking service.

www.initaly.com
An enthusiastic site run by passionate lovers of Italy from the US. It's packed with information and articles about the country, with quirky tips and insider stories, and makes excellent browsing when you're planning your trip.

www.hotelme.it
A user-friendly hotel booking service, with good coverage of Milan. Previous visitors share opinions and tips. English version available.

www.turismocremona.it/www.turismo.bergamo.it/ www.lakecomo.com
Official websites for Cremona, Bergamo and Lake Como. All have English versions.

www.fodors.com
A complete travel-planning site. You can research prices and weather; book air tickets, cars and rooms; pose questions to (and get answers from) fellow travelers; and find links to other sites.

www.atm-mi.it
Milan's city transport system runs this informative site, where you'll find everything you could possibly want to know, including how to buy the best ticket for your needs—Italian and English.

www.ferroviedellostato.it
The official site of the Italian State Railways, with excellent train information.

Accessing the internet on your mobile phone can be expensive, depending on what country you are from and your service provider. Most hotels offer wireless internet access, usually free, though sometimes only in the lobby area. The city launched Open Wifi in 2012, offering free public wifi in many central piazzas and streets, and in some museums, libraries and civic offices. To log in, you will need to register your mobile phone number. See www. turismo.milano.it

Getting There

ENTRY REQUIREMENTS

For the latest passport and visa information, look up the British embassy website at www.britishembassy.gov.uk, the United States embassy at www.americanembassy. com/europe, or for Canadians, travel.gc.ca.

INSURANCE

Check the cover provided by your insurance policy and buy any necessary supplements. EU nationals receive reduced-cost emergency medical treatment with the relevant documentation (EHIC for British residents), but travel insurance is still advised.

CUSTOMS REGULATIONS

EU nationals do not have to declare goods imported for their personal use.
The limits for non-EU visitors are 200 cigarettes or 100 small cigars or 250g of tobacco; 1 liter of alcohol (over 22 per cent alcohol) or 2 liters of fortified wine; 50g of perfume.

AIRPORTS

There are direct flights from all over the world into Malpensa airport, Milan's main international gateway, while Linate airport, classed as a city airport, handles just Italian domestic and European flights. Visitors from Europe can also arrive by rail or by bus.

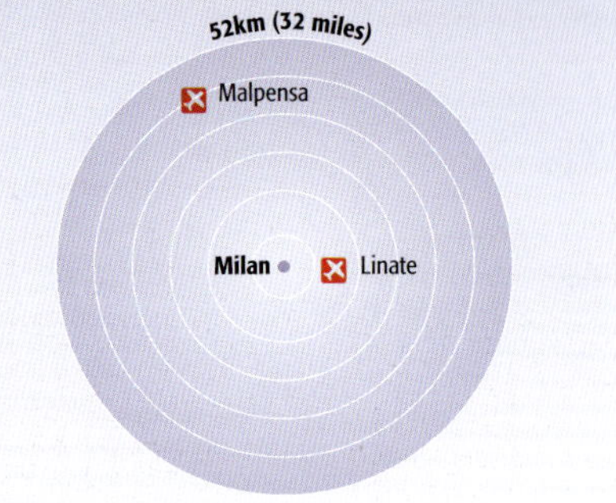

FROM MALPENSA

Most flights arrive at Malpensa, 50km (31 miles) northwest of the city (☎ 02 7845 2200; www. sea-aeroportimilano.it). The Malpensa Express train (☎ 02 8511 4382) runs to Cadorna–Ferrovie Nord (every 30 minutes, 6.53am–9.53pm; €11, journey time 40 minutes). You need to stamp your ticket in the machine located on the platform before boarding the train. The Malpensa Bus Express (☎ 02 3311 0794; www.malpensaexpress.it) leaves from outside the terminal to Stazione Centrale (every 30 minutes, 6.35am–11.35pm; €12, journey time 50–60 minutes). Malpensa Shuttle (☎ 02 5858 3185; www.malpensashuttle.it) operates a shuttle bus to Stazione Centrale (every 20 minutes, 5.30am–1am; €10, journey time 50–60 minutes). Taxis to the city can take up to 75 minutes depending on the traffic and are expensive (€75–€100). Make sure you get an official white taxi. If someone approaches you offering a taxi be aware this will cost you more. Taxis returning to Malpensa should display a sticker *"taxi autorizzato per il servizio aeroportuale lombardo"* on the screen.

FROM LINATE

Linate, the closest airport, is only 6km (4 miles) east of the city (☎ 02 7845 2200; www. sea-aeroportimilano.it). The most convenient option for getting into the city is by taxi; official white cabs line up outside the terminal (€25, but check the cost before). ATM city bus No. 73 (every 20 minutes, 6.35am–1.05am; journey time 25 minutes) goes to Piazza San Babila (tickets €1 from vending machines). STAM coach service run a service to Stazione Centrale (every 30 minutes, 5.40am– 9.35pm; €5; journey time 25 minutes).

ARRIVING BY BUS

The majority of domestic and international buses arrive at the main terminus in Piazza Castello. Autostradale Viaggi is the major bus company connecting Milan with the rest of Italy.

ARRIVING BY CAR

It is not advisable to drive into Central Milan. The city is divided into segments with a one-way system and you can only enter the city at a limited number of points. The "Sosta Milano" parking system is extremely difficult to understand and unless you have parking at your hotel it is really better not to use a car. If you do bring a car be aware that fuel stations in the city close for lunch, on Saturday afternoons and all day Sunday. Do not leave your car on yellow lines or in areas marked by a tow-away symbol. The bottom line is you are far better off using the excellent public transport system.

ARRIVING BY RAIL

Most international and domestic trains arrive at Stazione Centrale, in the northeast of the city, although the Malpensa Express arrives at Cardona–Ferrovie Nord, closer to the city center. There are easy connections to the rest of the city from here: The station is on Metro lines 2 and 3, taxis line up outside the entrance, and several trams and buses stop right outside.

In the land of the Vespa, it's tempting to hire a scooter (*motorino*) and Milan has many scooter rental outlets. But scooters are not for the fainthearted, and if you've never ridden one in a big city, Milan is not the place to start.

● **British Consulate**
✉ Via San Paulo 7
☎ 02 4220 2431
🕓 Mon–Fri 9.30–12.30, 2–4
● **US Consulate**
✉ Via Principe Amedeo 2/10
☎ 02 290 351
🕓 Mon–Fri 8.30–5.30
● **Canadian Consulate**
✉ Piazza Cavour 3
☎ 02 6269 4238
🕓 Mon–Fri 9–1; email before visiting: consul. canada.milan@gmail.com

Getting Around

Milan has an efficient integrated transportation system comprising trams, buses and a Metro, which is easy to use (www.atm-mi.it).

BUSES AND TRAMS

Bus and tram routes cover the whole city and also follow the Metro routes overground. Both are very efficient and run about every 10 minutes. They do get crowded, especially during rush hour—take care of your belongings. Bus and tram stops have a yellow sign displaying the route and a timetable. All buses and trams in Milan are orange except for the tourist trams, which are one of the best ways of seeing the city.

THE METRO

The Metro is the easiest and fastest option, though you may have to combine it with a bus or tram. The Metro consists of four lines: red MM1, green MM2, yellow MM3 and blue *passante ferroviario* (suburban loop). These intersect at the hub stations of Stazione Centrale, Duomo, Cardorna and Loreto.

TICKETS

Tickets must be purchased in advance and stamped in a machine once on board. Fines are handed out to anyone caught without a ticket. A single (€1.50) is valid for 90 minutes from validation and can be used on the entire system for as many bus and tram trips as you want, plus one Metro journey (a carnet of 10 tickets is available at €13.80). One- and two-day travel cards (€4.50/€8.25) are also available. These last 24/48 hours respectively from time of first stamping; once stamped you do not need to do it again. Tickets are sold at tobacconists, bars, newsstands, tourist offices and Metro stations. The network runs 6am–midnight, with night buses continuing until 1.30am.

TAXIS

Official taxis in Milan are normally white and the charges are reasonable. It is almost impossible to hail a passing cab so it's best to call

(Radiotaxi ☎ 02 4040; 02 8585; 02 6969) when you want one—they usually arrive quite quickly—or go to a taxi rank (stand) at Piazza del Duomo, Stazione Centrale, Piazza della Scala, Piazza San Babila, Piazza Diaz and Via Manzoni.

SCOOTERS, MOPEDS AND BICYCLES

Even experienced riders or cyclists should be careful if using this mode of transport on Milan's congested roads. There are several places in the city that hire these forms of transport: try Bianco Blu (✉ Via Gallarate 33 ☎ 02 3082 2430; www.biancoblu.com) for scooters and mopeds; AWS (✉ Via Ponte Seveso 33 ☎ 02 6707 2145) for bicycles.

WALKING

Walking is the best way to get around, but do beware of chaotic traffic when crossing the road.

ORGANIZED SIGHTSEEING

A bus tour, run by Autostradale (☎ 02 3391 0749), leaves Piazza Duomo (Tue–Sun 9.30am) for a three-hour tour to most of Milan's main sights, accompanied by a multilingual commentary; cost €55 including pick-up and drop-off at selected hotels and entrance fees. For a fascinating overview of the city take the City Sightseeing Milano bus (☎ 02 867 131; www.city-sightseeing.it)—two different hop-on hop-off guided tours with multilingual recorded commentary. It departs from Piazza Castello (daily all year; tours leave 9.30–5.45; 6.30 in summer) and lasts for about 1 hour 30 minutes; cost €25; reduced cost for children (5–15 years) €10. You can buy tickets for both tours at the tourist information offices.

An alternative is to view the city on foot. Walking Tours of Milan (Via Marconi 1 ☎ 02 7252 4301) run a tour every Monday from the APT tourist office. A Friend in Milan (☎ 02 2952 0570; www.friendinmilan.co.uk) provides guided walking tours throughout the city.

Essential Facts

MONEY

The euro (€) is the official currency of Italy. Banknotes are in denominations of 5, 10, 20, 50, 100, 200 and 500 euros, and coins in denominations of 1, 2, 5, 10, 20, 50 cents and 1 and 2 euros. Credit cards are widely accepted and most banks have ATMs.

WOMEN VISITORS

● Women are generally safe visiting Milan alone.
● After dark avoid Parco Sempione, the rail station and poorly lit streets away from the middle of the city.

ELECTRICITY

● Voltage is 220 volts and sockets take two round pins.

LOST PROPERTY

● Council lost property office ✉ Via Friuli 30 ☎ 02 8845 3908/9 🕒 Mon–Fri 8.30–4
● Central railway left luggage office ✉ Stazione Centrale (1st floor of Galleria Partenze) ☎ 02 6371 2667 🕒 Daily 6am–1am
● It is imperative to report losses of passports to the police (▷ Emergency Numbers panel, opposite).

MAIL

● General post office information ☎ 803 160, www.poste.it.
● Main post office ✉ Via Cordusio 4 ☎ 02 7248 2126 🕒 Mon–Fri 8–7, Sat 8.30–12.
● There is another big post office at the Stazione Centrale ✉ Via Sammartini ☎ 02 669 2467 🕒 Mon–Fri 8–7, Sat 8.30–9.
● You can buy stamps (*francobolli*) from post offices or from tobacconists displaying a white T sign on a dark background.
● Post boxes are small, red and marked *Poste* or *Lettere*. The slot on the left is for addresses within the city and the slot on the right is for other destinations.

MEDICINES AND MEDICAL TREATMENT

● Medical emergencies ☎ 118 or go to the *Pronto Soccorso* (casualty department or emergency room) of the nearest hospital.
● Poison Antidote Centre ☎ 02 6610 1029.
● Pharmacies are indicated by a large green or red cross.
● There is a free emergency number giving details of your nearest pharmacy ☎ 800 801 185. The Central Station pharmacy is open 24 hours a day, in the first floor departures gallery.
● There are several night pharmacies, including those located in: Piazza Duomo 21 ☎ 02 287 8668; Via Boccaccio 26 ☎ 02 469 5281; Corso Magenta 96 ☎ 02 4800 6772.

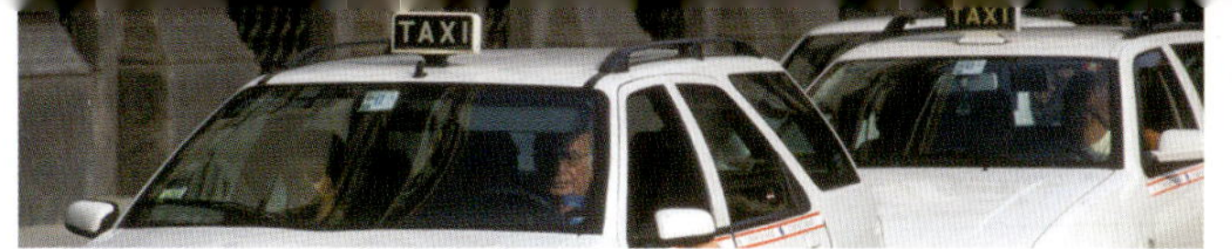

OPENING TIMES

- Banks: Mon–Fri 8.30–1.30, 3–4.
- Post offices: Mon–Fri 8.30–1.50, Sat 8–12. The main city post offices stay open at lunchtime and close at 7.
- Shops: normally 9.30–1, 3.30–7.30.
- Museums: see individual entries.
- Churches: 7 or 8–12.30, 3 or 4–7.30. Main tourist attractions often stay open longer. No two are the same.

PUBLIC HOLIDAYS

1 Jan: New Year's Day; 6 Jan: Epiphany; Easter Sunday; Easter Monday; 25 Apr: Liberation Day; 1 May: Labor Day; 2 Jun: Republic Day; 15 Aug: Assumption; 1 Nov: All Saints' Day; 8 Dec: Immaculate Conception; 25 Dec: Christmas Day; 26 Dec: St. Stephen's Day. Most places of interest close on New Year's Day, 1 May and Christmas, while others close on all public holidays.

TELEPHONES

- There are few telephone centers in the city: Galleria Vittorio Emanuele II 🕾 Daily 8am–9.30pm; Stazione Centrale 🕾 Daily 9am–9.30pm.
- Phone cards (*carta, scheda or tessera telefonica*) are the most practical way to use a public phone as few public telephones take coins.
- Directory enquiries 🕾 12.
- International directories 🕾 176.
- International operator 🕾 170.
- Cheap rate is all day Sunday and 9pm–8am (national) on other days; 10pm–8am (international).
- To call Italy from the UK, dial 00 followed by 39 (the code for Italy) then the number. To call the UK from Italy dial 00 44 then drop the first zero from the area code.
- To call Italy from the US dial 011 followed by 39. To call the US from Italy dial 00 1.
- Milan's area code (02) must be dialed even if you are calling from within the city.

EMERGENCY NUMBERS

- Police 🕾 113
- Police (Carabinieri) 🕾 112
- Police headquarters (for foreigners and passport office) ✉ Via Montebello 26 🕾 02 62261
- Fire 🕾 115
- Ambulance 🕾 118
- Breakdown service Automobile Club di Milano (ACI) 🕾 803 116

NEWSPAPERS

The daily city newspaper, *Il Corriere*, includes listings for plays, music and cinema. Other Italian dailies, *La Repubblica* and *Corriere della Sera*, produce weekly supplements with up-to-date listings of cultural events in the city. The tourist office has a free newspaper, *Hello Milano*, in English, giving information and listings on the arts, plays, nightlife and a little on shopping, and *Milanomese*, with listings of what's on.
Foreign newspapers can usually be bought after about 2.30 on the day of issue from booths (*edicole*) in the city. European editions of the *Financial Times*, *USA Today* and *International Herald Tribune* are also available.

Language

All Italian words are pronounced as written, with each vowel and consonant sounded. Only the letter *h* is silent, but it modifies the sound of other letters. The letter *c* is hard, as in English "cat", except when followed by *i* or *e*, when it becomes the soft *ch* of "cello". Similarly, *g* is soft (as in the English "giant") when followed by *i* or *e*—*giardino*, *gelati*; otherwise hard (as in "gas")—*gatto*. Words ending in *o* are almost always masculine in gender (plural: *-i*); those ending in *a* are generally feminine (plural: *-e*). Use the polite second person (*lei*) to speak to strangers and the informal second person (*tu*) to friends or children.

USEFUL WORDS	
yes	*sì*
no	*no*
please	*per favore*
thank you	*grazie*
you're welcome	*prego*
excuse me!	*scusi*
where	*dove*
here	*qui*
there	*là*
when	*quando*
now	*adesso*
later	*più tardi*
why	*perchè*
who	*chi*
may I/can I	*posso*
good morning	*buon giorno*
good afternoon/ good evening	*buona sera/ buona notte*
hello/good-bye (informal)	*ciao*
hello (on the telephone)	*pronto*
I'm sorry	*mi dispiace*
left/right	*sinistra/destra*
open/closed	*aperto/chiuso*
good/bad	*buono/cattivo*
big/small	*grande/piccolo*
with/without	*con/senza*
more/less	*più/meno*
hot/cold	*caldo/freddo*
early/late	*presto/ritardo*
now/later	*adesso/più tardi*
today/tomorrow	*oggi/domani*
when?/do you have?	*quando?/avete?*

NUMBERS	
1	*uno, una*
2	*due*
3	*tre*
4	*quattro*
5	*cinque*
6	*sei*
7	*sette*
8	*otto*
9	*nove*
10	*dieci*
20	*venti*
30	*trenta*
40	*quaranta*
50	*cinquanta*
100	*cento*
1,000	*mille*

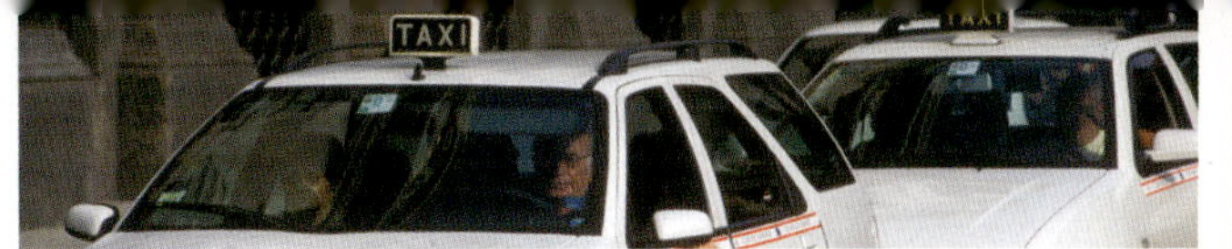

EMERGENCIES

help!	*aiuto!*
stop, thief!	*al ladro!*
can you help me, please?	*può aiutarmi, per favore?*
call the police/an ambulance	*chiami la polizia/ un'ambulanza*
I have lost my wallet/ passport	*ho perso il mio passaporto/ il mio portafoglio*
where is the police station?	*dov'è il commissariato?*
where is the hospital?	*dov'è l'ospedale?*
I don't feel well	*non mi sento bene*
first aid	*pronto soc corso*

COLOURS

black	*nero*
brown	*marrone*
pink	*rosa*
red	*rosso*
orange	*arancia*
yellow	*giallo*
green	*verde*
light blue	*celeste*
sky blue	*azzuro*
purple	*viola*
white	*bianco*
gray	*grigio*

USEFUL PHRASES

how are you? (informal)	*come sta/stai?*
I'm fine	*sto bene*
I do not understand	*non ho capito*
how much is it?	*quant'è?*
do you have a room?	*avete camere libere?*
how much per night?	*quanto costa una notte?*
with bath/shower	*con bagno/doccia*
when is breakfast served?	*a che ora è servita la colazione?*
where is the train/ bus station?	*dov'è la stazione ferroviaria degli autobus?*
where are we?	*dove siamo?*
do I have to get off here?	*devo scendere qui?*
I'm looking for ...	*cerco...*
where can I buy ...?	*dove posso comprare...?*
a table for ... please	*un tavolo per... per favore*
can I have the bill?	*il conto*
we didn't have this	*non abbiamo avuto questo*
where are the toilets?	*dove sono i gabinetti?*

DAYS/MONTHS

Monday	*lunedì*
Tuesday	*martedì*
Wednesday	*mercoledì*
Thursday	*giovedì*
Friday	*venerdì*
Saturday	*sabato*
Sunday	*domenica*
January	*gennaio*
February	*febbraio*
March	*marzo*
April	*aprile*
May	*maggio*
June	*giugno*
July	*luglio*
August	*agosto*
September	*settembre*
October	*ottobre*
November	*novembre*
December	*dicembre*

Timeline

NAPOLEON'S RULE

The city of Milan welcomed the arrival of Napoleon, and indeed it was he who brought forward the idea of the unification of Italy. His contributions to the city included reforming the educational and legal system, inaugurating the building of new public offices and establishing new museums and art galleries. He even saw the completion of the Duomo so he could hold his coronation there as the self-appointed "king of Italy". However, after 18 years of rule and high taxation the Milanese people were relieved when Napoleon was defeated at the Battle of Waterloo and Milan was returned to Habsburg rule.

From left to right: Milan's awesome cathedral; detail of a statue at the Castello Sforzesco; relaxing in the grounds of the castle; gloriously illuminated—the Duomo at night

222BC The Romans defeat the Gauls. Milan becomes the most important city in the Western Roman Empire after Rome.

AD374 Sant'Ambrogio (St. Ambrose) becomes Bishop of Milan. The city flourishes.

452 The city is devastated by Attila the Hun, then again in 489 by the Goths.

568 Lombards invade and take power.

774 Rebirth of the city under the rule of Charlemagne.

1042 Milan becomes an autonomous city.

1162 German Emperor Frederick I invades. Milan is burned to the ground.

1176 Battle of Legnano gives independence to northern Italian cities.

1277 Rise of the Visconti family. The Duomo is commissioned in 1386.

1450 Rise of the Sforza family; for 50 years art and commerce flourish.

1499 Louis XII of France occupies Milan.

1540–1706 Milan under Spanish rule.

1706 Control of the city passes to the Austrian Habsburgs.

1796–1814 Napoleonic rule. New building work is undertaken.

1804 Napoleon's coronation at the Duomo.

1815 Napoleon is defeated and Milan is handed back to the Habsburgs.

1848 Unification—Milan becomes part of Italy. The population increases to 240,000.

1919 Fascist movement founded by Benito Mussolini in Milan.

1939–1945 Milan suffers serious bomb damage during World War II.

1950s Milan leads Italy's economic recovery.

1960s Industrial and student unrest. Acts of terrorism take place.

1990s Corruption and political scandal rife; Milan becomes known as "bribe" city.

2004 La Scala Opera House opens after three years of closure for restoration.

2012 The innovative Bosco Verticale (Vertical Forest) residential towers open near Porta Garibaldi, with 900 trees and shrubs growing on a series of terraces up the outsides.

2013 Silvio Berlusconi is convicted of tax fraud and expelled from the Italian senate.

During the Bronze Age, the Ligurians were the first to settle in the Po Valley, and by the sixth century BC the powerful Etruscans were well ensconced. By 338–386BC, after various skirmishes, the area was ruled by the Gauls.

The patron saint of Milan, whose feast day is on 7 December, was Bishop of Milan from AD374–397. As a result of his integrity and skill in negotiating between the Catholic and Arian church officials, Milan became an important religious hub.

Index

Published by AA Publishing, a trading name of AA Media Limited, whose registered office is Fanum House, Basing View, Basingstoke, Hampshire RG21 4EA. Registered number 06112600.

© **AA Media Limited 2016**
First published 2005
New edition 2016

WRITTEN BY Jackie Staddon and Hilary Weston
UPDATED BY Barbara Rogers
SERIES EDITOR Clare Ashton
DESIGN WORK Tracey Freestone
IMAGE RETOUCHING AND REPRO Ian Little

Colour separation by AA Digital Department
Printed and bound by Leo Paper Products, China

A CIP catalogue record for this book is available from the British Library.

ISBN 978-0-7495-7802-2

A05378
Maps in this title produced from mapping © MAIRDUMONT / Falk Verlag 2012 and data from openstreetmap.org © OpenStreetMap contributors
Transport map © Communicarta Ltd, UK

The Automobile Association would like to thank the following photographers, companies and picture libraries for their assistance in the preparation of this book.

4/18t AA/M Jourdan; **4tl** AA/C Sawyer; **5** AA/C Sawyer; **6cl** AA/M Jourdan; **6c** AA/C Sawyer; **6cr** AA/M Jourdan; **6bl** AA/M Jourdan; **6bcl** AA/M Jourdan; **6bcr** Photodisc; **6br** Photodisc; **7cl** Fototeca ; **7c** AA/M Jourdan; **7cr** AA/C Sawyer; **7bl** AA/J Tims; **7bc** AA/P Bennett; **7br** Brand X Pics; **10tr** AA/M Jourdan; **10tcr** AA/M Jourdan; **10cr** AA/M Jourdan; **10/11br** AA/M Jourdan; **11tl** AA/M Jourdan; **11tcl** AA/M Jourdan; **11cl** AA/C Sawyer; **13tl** AA/C Sawyer; **13tcl** Archivio Fotografico I.A.T. Ufficio Informazioni e Accoglienza Turistica della Provincia di Milano palcoreale; **13cl** Brand X Pics; **13bcl** Digitalvision; **13bl** Brand X Pics; **14tr** David Wasserman/brandxpictures; **14tcr** AA/M Jourdan; **14cr** AA/M Jourdan; **14br** AA/S McBride; **15bl** AA/M Jourdan; **16tr** AA/M Jourdan; **16cr** AA/M Jourdan; **16br** AA/C Sawyer; **17tl** AA/C Sawyer; **17tcl** AA/C Sawyer; **17cl** AA/J Holmes; **17bl** AA/J Holmes; **18tr** AA/M Jourdan; **18tcr** Museo Nazionale della Scienza e della Tecnologia; **18cr** AA/M Jourdan; **18br** Brand X Pics; **19(i)** AA/C Sawyer; **19(ii)** AA/C Sawyer; **19(iii)** AA/P Bennett; **19(iv)** Museo Nazionale della Scienza e della Tecnologia; **19(v)** AA/P Bennett; **20/21** AA/M Jourdan; **24tl** AA/M Jourdan; **24tr** AA/M Jourdan; **25tl** AA/M Jourdan; **25tr** AA/M Jourdan; **26t** The Bridgeman Art Library; **27tl** AA/M Jourdan; **27tr** Alinari Archives; **28l** AA/M Jourdan; **28/29** AA/M Jourdan; **29r** AA/M Jourdan; **30/31** Alinari Archives; **32–33t** AA/M Jourdan; **32bl** © Stock Italia/Alamy; **32br** AA/M Jourdan; **33b** Seat Archive/Alinari Archives; **34t** AA/M Jourdan; **35t** AA/M Jourdan; **36t** AA/M Jourdan; **37t** AA/M Jourdan; **38t** Digitalvision; **39t** AA/C Sawyer; **40** AA/T Harris; **41** AA/M Jourdan; **44tl** AA/M Jourdan; **44/45t** AA/M Jourdan; **44bl** AA/M Jourdan; **44bc** AA/M Jourdan; **44/45b** AA/M Jourdan; **45r** AA/M Jourdan; **46l** AA; **46/47tr** AA/C Sawyer; **46cr** AA/M Jourdan; **47tr** AA/M Jourdan; **47cl** AA/M Jourdan; **47cr** AA/M Jourdan; **48tl** AA/M Jourdan; **48tr** AA/M Jourdan; **49l** Valentino Visentini/Alamy; **49r** HermesMereghetti/Alamy; **50tl** © World Pictures/Alamy; **50tr** Archivio Fotografico I.A.T. Ufficio Informazioni e Accoglienza Turistica della Provincia di Milano; **51t** The Bridgeman Art Library; **52tl** www.vittorebuzzi.it/Alamy; **52tr** AA/C Sawyer; **53** © Clive Tully/Alamy; **54–55t** AA/M Jourdan; **54b** AA/M Jourdan; **55bl** AA/M Jourdan; **55br** © World Pictures/Alamy; **56t** AA/M Jourdan; **57t** AA/C Sawyer; **58t** AA/M Chaplow; **58c** Photodisc; **59t** AA/E Meacher; **60t** David Wasserman/brandxpictures; **61** AA/M Jourdan; **64** © CuboImages srl/Alamy; **65tl** AA/M Jourdan; **65tc** AA/M Jourdan; **65tr** AA/M Jourdan; **66l** AA/M Jourdan; **66/67tr** AA/M Jourdan; **66cr** AA/M Jourdan; **67tr** AA/P Bennett; **67bl** AA/P Bennett; **67bc** AA/M Jourdan; **67br** AA/M Jourdan; **68l** Alain Machet (3)/Alamy; **68tr** AA/M Jourdan; **69** AA/M Jourdan; **70** © World Pictures / Alamy; **71t** Seat Archive/Alinari Archives; **72tl** Alinari Archives; **72/73tr** AA/M Jourdan; **72cl** AA/C Sawyer; **72cr** AA/M Jourdan; **73r** AA/C Sawyer; **73cl** AA/C Sawyer; **74t** AA/M Jourdan; **74b** AA/M Jourdan; **75t** AA/M Jourdan; **76t** Photodisc; **77t** Brand X Pics; **78t** AA/A Kouprianoff; **79** AA/M Jourdan; **82/83** Seat Archive/Alinari Archives; **83tr** Seat Archive/Alinari Archives; **83cr** AA/M Jourdan; **84l** Museo Nazionale della Scienza e della Tecnologia; **84/85tr** Museo Nazionale della Scienza e della Tecnologia; **84cr** Museo Nazionale della Scienza e della Tecnologia; **85tr** Museo Nazionale della Scienza e della Tecnologia; **85cl** Museo Nazionale della Scienza e della Tecnologia; **85cr** Museo Nazionale della Scienza e della Tecnologia; **86tl** AA/M Jourdan; **86tr** AA/M Jourdan; **87** AA/M Jourdan; **88t** AA/M Jourdan; **88bl** Archivio Fotografico I.A.T. Ufficio Informazioni e Accoglienza Turistica della Provincia di Milano; **88br** AA/C Sawyer; **89t** AA/M Jourdan; **90t** AA/M Jourdan; **91t** Digitalvision; **92t** AA/T Souter; **93** AA/P Bennett; **96t** H P Merten/Robert Harding; **97tl** AA/M Jourdan; **97tr** The Bridgeman Art Library; **98–99t** AA/M Jourdan; **98b** Società Trenno Ippodromi di San Siro; **99b** © Dyana/Alamy; **100–101t** AA/C Sawyer; **100bl** AA/M Jourdan; **100br** AA/A Mockford & N Bonetti; **101bl** AA/M Jourdan; **101bc** AA/C Sawyer; **101br** AA/P Bennett; **102** AA/C Sawyer; **103t** Digitalvision; **104t** Brand X Pics; **105t** AA/S McBride; **106t** AA/M Jourdan; **107** AA/C Sawyer; **108–112t** AA/C Sawyer; **108tr** AA/A Mockford & N Bonetti; **108tcr** Stockbyte; **108cr** Photodisc; **108br** AA/C Sawyer; **113** AA/M Jourdan; **114–125t** AA/M Jourdan; **119cr** AA/M Jourdan; **119br** AA/M Jourdan; **120bl** AA/J Edmanson; **121cr** AA/M Jourdan; **122cr** AA/M Jourdan; **124bl** AA; **124br** AA/M Jourdan; **125bl** AA/P Bennett; **125br** AA/C Sawyer

Every effort has been made to trace the copyright holders, and we apologize in advance for any accidental errors. We would be happy to apply the corrections in the following edition of this publication.

Titles in the Series

- Amsterdam
- Bangkok
- Barcelona
- Berlin
- Boston
- Brussels & Bruges
- Budapest
- Dublin
- Edinburgh
- Florence
- Hong Kong
- Istanbul
- Las Vegas
- Lisbon
- London
- Madrid
- Milan
- Munich
- New York
- Orlando
- Paris
- Prague
- Rome
- San Francisco
- Singapore
- Sydney
- Toronto
- Venice
- Vienna
- Washington